*Cruel Tears*

# CRUEL TEARS

**Ken Mitchell and Humphrey & the Dumptrucks**

Vancouver, Talonbooks, 1977

published with assistance from the Canada Council

*Talonbooks*
*201 1019 East Cordova,*
*Vancouver*
*British Columbia V6A 1M8*
*Canada*

This book was typeset by Linda Gilbert of B.C. Monthly
Typesetting Service, designed by David Robinson and printed
in Canada by Hignell Printing Limited

The text photographs were taken by Glen E. Erikson.

First printing: May 1977
Second printing: June 1983
Third printing: August 1986
Fourth printing: February 1989

Canadian Cataloguing in Publication Data

Mitchell, Ken, 1940—
    Cruel tears

    A play.
    ISBN 0-88922-120-0

    I. Humphrey & the Dumptrucks (Musical group).
    II. Title.
PS8576       C812'.5'4     C77-002128-X
PR9199.3

*for*
*Brian Richmond*
*Martha, Jaye, Bobby and Amy*
*Cory and Adam*
*Michael and Bear, Great Guys*

Acknowledgements:

*Geraldi Cinthio*
*William Shakespear*
*Brian Sklar*

*Cruel Tears* was commissioned by and first performed at Persephone Theatre in Saskatoon, Saskatchewan, on March 15, 1975, with the following cast:

| | |
|---|---|
| Johnny Roychuk | Winston Rekert |
| Kathy Jensen | Dorothy-Ann Haug |
| Jack Deal | David Stein |
| Florazarea (Flora) Deal | Janet Wright |
| Earl Jensen | Larry Ewashen |
| Ricky Yates | Robert J. Wright |
| Roy Carter | David Miller |
| Bartender | Larry Ewashen |
| Debbie Lou Belinsky | Janet Wright |
| Policeman | Larry Ewashen |
| Hitchhiker | Andrew Czaplejewski |
| Chorus | Marcella Cenaiko, Tamara Hrechuck, Andrew Nahachewsky, Thomas Nahachewsky |
| Vocal Chorus | Humphrey & the Dumptrucks |

Directed by Brian Richmond
Designed by Joan Paih and Gie Roberts
Choreographed by Bohdan E. Wowk
Music by Humphrey & the Dumptrucks

*Cruel Tears* was revived by Persephone Theatre in Saskatoon, Saskatchewan, on May 28, 1976, and subsequently played at the Vancouver East Cultural Centre in Vancouver, B.C., where it opened on June 8, 1976 as part of Festival Habitat, and at Centaur Theatre in Montréal, Québec, where it opened July 5, 1976 as part of the XXI Olympics. The cast was as follows:

| | |
|---|---|
| Johnny Roychuk | Winston Rekert |
| Kathy Jensen | Anne Wright |
| Jack Deal | Alex Diakun |
| Florazarea (Flora) Deal | Susan Wright |
| Earl Jensen | Wally Michaels |
| Ricky Yates | Robert J. Wright |
| Roy Carter | David Miller |
| Debbie Lou Belinsky | Karen Wiens |
| Filthy Phil | Wally Michaels |
| Policeman | Wally Michaels |
| Chorus | Marcella Cenaiko, Andrew Nahachewsky |
| Vocal Chorus | Humphrey & the Dumptrucks |

Directed by Brian Richmond
Designed by Doug Welch and Ted Roberts
Choreographed by Bohdan E. Wowk
Music by Humphrey & the Dumptrucks

## LIST OF CHARACTERS

JOHNNY ROYCHUCK, 28, *a truck driver.*
KATHY JENSEN, 19, *his sweetheart and wife.*
EARL JENSEN, 45, *owner of Motormack Express.*
JACK DEAL, 30, *Johnny's friend.*
FLORAZAREA (FLORA) DEAL, 30, *Jack's Wife.*
RICKY YATES, 22, *a driver.*
ROY CARTER, 40, *a driver.*
FILTHY PHIL, *a driver.*
DEBBIE LOU BELINSKY, 25-45, *a waitress.*
A POLICEMAN.
CHORUS, *dancers and mimes.*
VOCAL CHORUS, *three singers.*

## PLACE

Saskatoon, Saskatchewan.

## TIME

May-June, 1974.

## SET

*The stage is divided into four levels. Upstage right is the highest level, Level 1, a small platform which serves as the bedroom. Opposite, upstage left, is a platform at a slightly lower level, Level 2, where the VOCAL CHORUS stands. Between these two platforms, upstage, is the third level, Level 3. The lowest level, Level 4, the floor, roughly half the stage, is where most of the action and the larger scenes take place.*

# Act One

*The house lights are off; the stage is black. The VOCAL CHORUS begins to make the sound of the prairie wind moaning. The first chords of the "Overture" are heard. As the "Overture" is played, the lights come up slowly, suggesting the rise of a bright prairie sun in early May. The sound of a meadowlark trilling is heard. as the "Overture" reaches full tempo, the light becomes hot. A mime suggests a prairie environment. The "Overture" ends.*

*The VOCAL CHORUS sings "Cruel Tears Talking Blues."*

VOCAL CHORUS:
> *Well we got a song about the West,*
> *But we don't want you to get all depressed.*
> *Now it's all about people and it's kinda sad,*
> *'Cuz you know some are good and some are bad.*
>
> > *Call it "Cruel Tears."*
> > refrain *"Cruel Tears."*

*Like this land that we live in here,*
*Our story don't go too far to cheer,*
*But hear it even if yuh choke —*
*You might even know some of these folks.*
    *They're all country people.*
    *"Westerners"*
    *Like they say in Ottawa.  Wa.*

*We been through a lot, you and us,*
*We licked the winters and fought the dust,*
*We stuck the thirties up Bennett's ass.*
*Now we're waitin' for the time to pass,*
    *Good times we mean to say,*
    *Lookin' for 'em every day,*
    *But she's tough.*

*Why did they struggle, all of them years,*
*Breakin' their backs and cryin' cruel tears?*
*Looking for rain and chewing on dirt,*
*Schoolin' the kids so they don't get hurt.*
    *That's what it's all about —*
    *For the children.*
    *The future.*
    refrain *If it ever comes.*

*You know who's gonna change this world?*
*Those sunburned boys and blushing girls.*
*Doesn't feel right when they go away,*
*But farming these days don't seem to pay.*
    *So it's off to the city.*
    *High rise apartments.*
    *O.K. Economy.*

*You can make a bundle, if you don't get caught*
*Tearin' down homes for parking lots.*
*You meet a lot of people in the push and shove,*
*Tryin' to buy success, what they need is love.*
*(Too expensive!)*
    *City lights.*
    *Every night a party.*
    Good *times!*

*We're gonna show 'em at work and show 'em at play.*
*We'll show you the place where they spend their pay.*
*The men drive trucks and the girls keep house.*
*They do what they can, or they do without.*
    *Cruel Tears.*
    *Taste a little like whiskey.*
    *Hurtin' like sin.*

    *Cruel Tears!*

*The lights go up on Level 3 where JOHNNY*
*ROYCHUCK appears "driving" his truck.*
*He sings "The Lonesome Trucker Blues."*

JOHNNY:
    *Well, I been pushing this White Freightliner twenty hours,*
    *Take another twenty 'fore I stop.*
    *Log book says, "Take your time,"*
    *But on a day like this I'm flyin'*
    *And the only one I'm cheatin' is the clock.*

    *Drifting along under endless skies*
    *Racing my shadow down the road*
    *Born for courtin' danger,*
    *Often lonesome as a stranger,*
    *This diesel is my best friend and my home.*

    *The boys will all be waiting at the Blacktop.*
    *The harder we been workin', the rowdier we are.*
    *There'll be money in the jukebox,*
    *And boozin' till the door's locked,*
    *My friends'll all be waitin' at the bar.*

    *The lights go up on the Blacktop Bar. Instru-*
    *mental music continues in the background.*
    *JACK, RICKY and ROY have entered the bar.*
    *JACK is neat, handsome. ROY is old-fashioned,*
    *"straight." RICKY has long hair and fancy*
    *denims.*

ROY:

    You buyin' the first round, Jack?

JACK:

    This one's on me, boys!

RICKY:

    Yer lookin' perty fat, arnchuh?

    *To ROY.*

    Didjuh check the new chrome stacks on his Kenworth?

ROY:

    Hey, yuh gonna get a set of moon discs, eh, Jack?

JACK:

    Just cuz you were dumb enough to buy 'em for that old Jimmy a yours! And then lose one the next day at a railroad crossin'!

    *They laugh.*

RICKY:

    Yeah — but how about all that crummy red plastic you stuck inside yer cab? I keep seein' pieces of it blowin' down the ditches on Number Eleven!

JACK:

    Don't worry, hippie! It'll last longer'n that dumb shag carpeting in that gutless Mac of yours.

ROY:

    Yeah, he don't call it a shaggin' wagon fer nuthin'! Haw haw!

18

RICKY:
> Shaggin' wagon! You should talk!

> *To JACK.*

> Yuh know that redhead waitress at the Husky House?

JACK: *already laughing*
> Yeah.

RICKY:
> Guess whose truck I saw at six o'clock this morning, parked behind the gradge? Roy's!

ROY: *embarrassed, but pleased that they noticed*
> Awwwwww!

JACK:
> Yeah, but diddenchuh see? It wasn't the redhead he had in his bunk — it was the *Husky!*

> *They all laugh uproariously. Freeze. The lights dim on the bar.*

JOHNNY:
> *For a trucker there's no limit to the ladies.*
> *Some are easy goin' and some you can't get near.*
> *Married women are callin' in,*
> *Mona wonders, "Where you bin?"*
> *And Debbie Lou keeps layin' on the beer!*

> *The lights go up again on the bar. The instrumental music continues. There is a vacant chair for JOHNNY at the table in the bar.*

JACK: *calling to the back*
> Hey, Debbie — Loooooo! Quit waterin' the rye!
> Come on out here — we're all gettin' dry!

ROY:
> Yeah, gettin' thirsty!

RICKY:
Hey nurse! Time for my shot!

*DEBBIE LOU enters with a tray. She is heavily made up, still looking for her man. She could wear a very short skirt emblazoned with trucking crests.*

DEBBIE LOU:
Why don't I just bring the whole bar over here? You guys got hollow legs fer pourin' it down?

*The men laugh. FILTHY PHIL enters. His name refers to his style, not his hygiene. FILTHY PHIL has a wide repertoire of obscene words, gestures and leers.*

FILTHY PHIL:
Hey Debs, *I* got a hollow leg. Wanna see it?

DEBBIE LOU:  *right back*
Well, I hope it's bigger'n last time!

JACK:
Wanna check mine out for size?

DEBBIE LOU:
Well, I'd take a chance on anything — but *Mrs.* Deal might have somepin to say 'bout that.

ROY:
Haw haw. She got yuh there, Jack! She's lookin' for a *single* guy! Right, Debbie Lou?

DEBBIE LOU:
May be I'm not lookin' at all! I'm perty choosey, yuh know.

RICKY:  *shaking his locks*
Yeah — she's goin' for the dry look! Arnchuh, Debs?

20

DEBBIE LOU:
>You said it — dry behind the ears!

>*Laughter.*

JACK:
>Hey, yer in there like a dirty shirt, hippie!

ROY: *an old joke*
>We'll hafta trim your hair first though! Right, you guys?

>*He laughs by himself.*

FILTHY PHIL:
>No, no — she dozen want *Ricky*! She's savin' herself
>fer — Ole Roy!

>*Freeze.*

JOHNNY:
>*But life is pretty hollow if yuh haven't got a plan,*
>*And you never try to find that special one.*
>*Now there's a woman I can trust*
>*And all my travellin's just become*
>*A better way of gettin' close to home.*

RICKY:
>Hey Filthy! How come yer in so late?

FILTHY PHIL:
>Aaa, got held up by a couple a mothertruckin'
>Smokies — just outside a Chamberpail.

ROY:
>Juh see Johnny?

FILTHY PHIL:
>Naw, the big Yewkeranian was ahead a me! Must a
>bin in some kinda hurry — Mona said he only stopped
>there for a minute.

ROY:

    I don't believe it! One minute fer the Manitoba
    Muffin?

JACK:

    You better convoy down there and look after her,
    dummy!

DEBBIE LOU:

    You guys quit buggin' Roy. You go puttin' notions
    in that so-called brain a his and there's gonna be
    trouble!

FILTHY PHIL: *elbowing ROY*
Go on, Roy, now's yer chance!

    *The boys laugh, jabbing each other in the ribs.*

DEBBIE LOU:
Same again here, fellas?

JACK:

    Yeah, hit us again! Roy's round!

DEBBIE LOU: *pointing around the table*
Right. Eight and a juice, rye and a Seven . . .

    *Pointing to JACK.*

One M.G. . . .

    *Pointing to RICKY.*

Rum and Coke . . .

    *Pointing to FILTHY PHIL.*

Couple a Heidleburg, one Pil and a Blue and a Blue!

    *Pointing to ROY.*

ROY: *interrupting*
    And uh — yuh got a ride home fer after work — yet?

DEBBIE LOU: *not even listening*
    Hey, where's Johnny tonight?

      *Freeze.*

      *JOHNNY sings the last stanza of the song.*

JOHNNY:
    *The chair they're holding will have to wait.*
    *There's a prairie lady lookin' for me soon,*
    *With promise in her smile,*
    *That stays with me all the while*
    *I head this big old rig on back to Saskatoon.*

      *JOHNNY crosses to Level 1, where KATHY*
      *is waiting. As the instrumental music ends, he*
      *reaches her and the lights go black on Level 1.*
      *Everyone is drunker in the bar.*

ROY:
    Hey, it's ten o'clock! Thought yuh said Johnny was cummin'!

JACK: *snarling*
    He's comin'!

RICKY:
    Yeah? How do you know?

JACK:
    'Cause I make it my bizness to know!

RICKY:
    That must be why you're the boss, eh?

JACK:
    I ain't the boss!

RICKY:

Yer the union boss, arnchuh? Same thing.

> *JACK grabs RICKY, threatening. The others react.*

JACK:

We got no union at Motormack! And there isn't gonna be one as long as *I'm* around!

RICKY:  *placating him*

Okay, yer the spokesman!

ROY:

Yeah, we *elected* him spokesman, Rick.

RICKY:

Okay, spokesman, when are yuh gonna talk to old man Jensen about gettin' us that pay-raise?

JACK:

I'm lookin' after it.

FILTHY PHIL:

Yeah. Keep the faith, Ricky!

RICKY:

Faith's cheap. It's the foldin' green I need. I wanta put a C.B. in my cab and I got no bucks.

JACK:

Don't worry, hippie, you'll get what's comin' to yuh.

ROY:

Whatssat, Jack? Gonna give 'im a haircut?

> *He laughs by himself.*

JACK:  *to RICKY*

I'm way ahead of yuh, loverboy! I got an appointment to see Jensen tomorrow.

RICKY:
Well, be sure 'n' kiss his ass for *me*, eh?

JACK: *rising*
You wanna step outside and show us how it's done?

DEBBIE LOU: *intervening*
Hey Ricky — where'd all the music go?

Seductively.

Wanna plug my Wurlitzer?

RICKY: *hesitating, grinning*
Sure, Debs — whucha like to hear? "Our Song?"

DEBBIE LOU dances RICKY over to the "juke
box," clowning. ROY and FILTHY PHIL hoot
and laugh.

DEBBIE LOU:
G — 7.

RICKY plugs the "juke box." JACK remains
sitting at the table while the others dance with
DEBBIE LOU. Eventually, JACK joins in. They
sing "One More for the Women."

VOCAL CHORUS
AND RICKY:
*Well, it's one more for the women,*
*And one more for the road.*
*Gas my truck, wish me luck, it's time to go.*
*Tell old Debbie at the Blacktop Bar,*
*I ain't goin' all that far —*
*But I got a heavy load.*
*So give me one more for those women,*
*One more for the road.*

RICKY:

> Now I'm the kinda guy who likes to travel.
> My home is wherever I go.
> Women are found in damn near every town,
> That's something you oughta know.
> It always makes them cry
> When you gotta say good-bye,
> But when you gotta go, you gotta go.

ALL:

> Give me one more for the women,
> One more for the road.

RICKY:

> Let me get my rig out on the highway,
> I want to see those headlights glow.
> I'll be there with time to spare,
> You're gonna see my airhorn blow.
> The cops on Number One
> You know I keep them on the run.
> I ain't known for bein' slow.

ALL:

> So give me one more for those women,
> One more for the road.

RICKY:

> There's a chick waiting for me in Regina.
> And one 'bout halfway down the road.
> Lots of gals, good old pals,
> Best I've ever known.
> They'll back you up, when you're outta luck,
> True Knights of the Road.

ALL:

> Give me one more for those women,
> One more for the road.
> So give me one more for those women,
> And give me one more for the road.

*Everyone takes their drinks and sits down.*
*DEBBIE LOU goes out for more drinks.*

ROY:
 Wish ole Johnny was here.

FILTHY PHIL:
 Aa, he's out chasin' skirts! You know Roychuck!

JACK:
 Don't talk crap! I seen him dodge two weigh-scales
 one Friday tuh get here for the boozin'! He's comin'!

RICKY: *realizing something*
 Hey, I know where he is!

ROY: *now thoroughly drunk*
 He's gotta get here fer th' party.

JACK:
 Aaa, go slobber on Debbie, will yuh?

ROY: *blubbering*
 She dozzen wamme neither!

RICKY:
 He's got a girl friend!

JACK: *to RICKY*
 Aw, yer full of it! The last guy who's gonna get
 trapped up in this town is Johnny Roychuck!

RICKY:
 That's how much you know! This time he's *hooked*!

JACK:
 You wanna bet?

FILTHY PHIL:
 How 'bout it, hippie? Who is she?

*DEBBIE LOU re-enters.*

DEBBIE LOU:
Last call, boys.

RICKY: *delighted with himself*
Little — Kathy — Jensen!

FILTHY PHIL:
*Earl's kid?*

ROY: *stunned*
Kathy Jensen?

RICKY:
Yeah, he's took her out a couple a times. And last week she picked him up at the loading dock!

JACK:
*What?*

RICKY:
In the old man's station wagon!

ROY:
Well whuya know? Good ole Johnny!

*A big uproar. JACK slams his fist down angrily, knocking over some glasses. DEBBIE LOU squeals.*

RICKY:
Hey, watch out!

JACK:
That's a load a bull!

*JACK slams out the door. There is an awkward silence.*

FILTHY PHIL:
> What's with him?

RICKY:
> Aaa — just pissed off Johnny's havin' a good time.
> Jealous!

> *The bar lights flash off and on.*

ROY:
> Hey, lash call!

FILTHY PHIL:
> More beer, Debbie Lou!

RICKY:
> Let's have another song.

DEBBIE LOU:
> Too late. Juke box's awready shut off.

> *The men give catcalls and groans.*

FILTHY PHIL:
> Come on, sweet-thighs, yuh owe us a couple.

RICKY:
> How 'bout it, Debs? I'll give yuh a ride home if you
> let me plug it in.

ROY:
> Yeah — me too!

DEBBIE LOU:  *relenting*
> Oh, awright. But yuh gotta promise to keep *him* . . .

> *To ROY.*

> . . . in his cage.

> *She goes to the "juke box" below the VOCAL*
> *CHORUS.*

Which one?

ROY:

> A real *romaaaanic* song!

DEBBIE LOU: *decisively*
> B — 3.

> *The instrumental music for "The Love Duet"*
> *begins. The lights come up on the bedroom,*
> *Level 1, where JOHNNY and KATHY are*
> *together on the bed.*

JOHNNY:

> *Kathy, you know I'm not much with words.*
> *It's hard to say things how I mean 'em.*
> *When I look at you, those words don't ring true,*
> *And I'm the damn fool that just said 'em.*

KATHY:

> *Oh Johnny, words are only a screen.*
> *Fine talk is for lawyers and statesmen.*
> *What I see in your eyes makes speeches all lies.*
> *Just hold me all night till the morn'.*

JOHNNY:

> *But you know that I love you!*
> *Though I'm not worthy of you,*
> *'Cause I grew up somewhere on the wrong side of town.*
> *And your family won't want to*
> *Admit I'm the one to*
> *Put their baby in a wedding gown.*

KATHY:

> *Why waste our time on marriage and morals?*
> *Let's only try to be happy tonight.*
> *Don't try to possess me,*
> *Just lie and caress me,*
> *Why promise a future too bright?*
> *Just lie here and love me all night.*

TOGETHER:

> *Together we'll find a way.*

KATHY:

> *Let's take it day by day.*

JOHNNY:

> *Just tell me I am the one.*

TOGETHER:

> *And we've got the world on the run.*

> *An instrumental break as they rise from the bed.*

JOHNNY:

> *We got to make plans for a family wedding*
> *And think out our life together.*

KATHY:

> *I don't need a ring to prove I love you,*
> *Or stay with you through stormy weather.*

JOHNNY:

> *No, it's got to be done right,*
> *With a priest and a ring.*
> *Common law ain't the way I was taught.*
> *I'll go to your father and ask for his blessing.*
> *And then we can go tie the knot.*

KATHY:

>*It isn't that simple! When I get married,*
>*It's going to be forever.*
>*There's no turning back*
>*Or changing your mind.*
>*You must be sure from the start.*

JOHNNY:

>*That's just what I feel in my heart!*
>*I'll go right away to your father and say:*
>*I want your daughter's hand in marriage,*
>*And if he listens to me,*
>*He'll just have to see . . .*

KATHY:

>*He'll never consent to our wedding.*

>>*The lights come up as the sun rises. It is dawn.*

JOHNNY:

>*Let's go together and talk to him now.*
>*We don't have to wait anymore.*

KATHY:

>*Oh Johnny, I love you.*

JOHNNY:

>*And I — love you too.*

TOGETHER:

>*We don't have to wait anymore.*

JOHNNY:

>*It's our life that we're fighting for.*

TOGETHER:

>*Together we'll find a way.*
>*To face the world wide awake.*
>*People can say what they will.*
>*I will be here with you still.*

*An instrumental bridge.*

VOCAL CHORUS:
> *There the lovers stand,*
> *Making future plans.*
> *They will love each other,*
> *Come what may.*
> refrain *Come what may.*
>
> *They sing their love song,*
> *And nothing can go wrong.*
> *They will love each other.*
> *Come what may.*
> refrain *Come what may.*

> *The bedroom goes black. The instrumental music for "Jack's Soliloquy" begins. The lights come up on Level 3 — JACK DEAL's mobile home. FLORA DEAL enters from the back looking tired and harassed, yawning. She is in a housedress, and while she is sloppy and haggard, she was once an attractive woman.*

FLORA: *calling to the back*
Jack! Come on, Jack! Get outta bed. It's nine-thirty.

JACK: *off*
Hey — where's my shirt?

FLORA:
Right where you dropped it last night!

JACK: *entering, half dressed*
Fix me a Bromo, will yuh? I'm dyin'!

> *He puts on his shirt.*

Maybe yuh better throw some rye into it. I gotta sore throat.

FLORA:  *sweetly*
>How about some Drano?

JACK:
>Very funny.

FLORA:
>How come yuh hafta go in on a Saturday anyway?

JACK:
>Hafta see Earl about somethin'.

FLORA:
>Gonna ask him about the raise?

JACK:  *downing a Bromo*
>'At's confidential, Flora — you know that.

FLORA:
>Yuh got in perty late last night.

JACK:
>Yeah, well — you know.

>*He grins.*

>Friday night with the boys, eh?

FLORA:
>Johnny there?

JACK:
>Who wants to know?

FLORA:  *shrugs*
>Just askin'.

JACK:  *looking around*
>Wherejuh put my good jacket?

FLORA: *pointing*
Here.

JACK: *heading for the door*
You got anythin' on today?

FLORA:
Yeah sure. The Mayor's comin' for *tea*.

JACK:

Uh-huh. Well — just have supper ready by five, eh?
Wanna watch the Flyers tonight.

*Heading out the "door."*

And tell those kids to keep their goddamn tricycles
off the driveway!

*He goes out the front "door."*

JACK:

*Why is it always me has to look like the heavy?*
*Tryna do right for everybody —*
*What kinda thanks do I get?*
*What kinda thanks do I get?*

*A pause.*

*I work my butt off for two whole years*
*To get these guys organized.*
*And what sorta thanks do I get?*
*A union couldn't a got 'em what I got 'em:*
*Decent contracts, weekends off.*
*And what kinda thanks do I get?*

*All y'hear about is Johnny.*
*Johnny. Johnny does this.*
*Johnny does that.*
*Come have a beer with us, Johnny!*

*An instrumental break.*

*Kathy Jensen, that stuck-up bitch!*
*Big Johnny — the truck drivers' hero!*
*The big bohunk and the boss's daughter!*

*An instrumental break.*

*Well Johnny, friends can help you out,*
*And Jack's yer buddy, realize it or not.*
*Realize it or not.*
*Okay kid, so you're naive.*
*Dumb as a gopher.*
*You got no idea what women can do.*
*You just don't understand 'em.*
*Just don't understand.*

*An instrumental break.*

*You did okay for a while though,*
*Didn't yuh? Eh?*
*It's always you quiet guys get the most.*
*You and Ricky. The pretty boys.*
*I wonder about Flora, the way she talks . . .*
*Prob'ly got it on with both of 'em.*
*Well, good for them!*
*Good for her!*

*An instrumental break.*

*I got more bedrooms on the road*
*Than she ever even dreamed about.*
*Give 'em the old killer smile — boom!*
*Jack Deal scores another chicken.*
*Chalk up another kill*
*On the side of his cab.*

*Johnny Roychuck. The boss's daughter.*
*Just like that — sellin' out the boys.*
*Well, one a these days, he'll thank me.*
*One a these days he'll thank me.*

*The music ends. The lights go up on EARL JENSEN working inside at his desk. JACK knocks at his "door."*

EARL:
Yeah — who is it?

JACK: *stepping inside*
Yuh free for a minnit, Mr. Jensen?

EARL:
What's on your mind, Deal?

JACK:
It's about the contract, Mr. Jensen.

EARL:
Contract talks are in September. You better see me then.

JACK:
Well, the boys are havin' it pretty tough with all this inflation. Cost a livin's goin' up alla time!

EARL:
Cost? Don't tell *me* about cost!

*He shows JACK the clipboard he has been working on.*

There's the fuel bill for this outfit last month.

*JACK looks. He whistles sympathetically.*

That's right — you guys never see it from my viewpoint.

JACK:
How about *our* viewpoint? We gotta *live*. It isn't just a matter of balancin' books, you know. We got kids to feed —

EARL:

> Every driver in the company signed that contract —!

JACK:

> Yeah, we signed, Mr. Jensen, but if it means we
> hafta work to rule just to get our fair share — well —

EARL:

> That sounds like *union* talk to me, Deal.

JACK:

> No unions here, Mr. Jensen.

EARL:

> That's right. Your job was to keep the Teamsters *out*.

JACK:

> Yeah — okay.

> *He shrugs and grins.*

> Can't blame a guy for tryin'. We gotta keep the boys
> happy, don't we?

EARL: *getting out a bottle of whiskey*
> That's right, Deal. Humour the boys. Have a slug?

JACK:

> Say no more!

> *EARL pours a drink for JACK. A pause.*
> *JACK toasts him.*

> Well — management wins again!

> *JACK laughs and drinks. EARL turns back to*
> *his work waiting for JACK to leave. JACK sets*
> *his glass down.*

EARL:

> What now?

40

JACK:

Well. I uh — don't know how to start — I'm not very good at talking about this kinda thing — I guess it's best to just come right to the point, not beat around the bush —

EARL:

What's the problem now?

JACK:

Oh, there's no problem — with the company. It's uh sorta — personal — matter.

EARL: *indignant*
Personal?

JACK:

Yuh see, there's this — talk goin' around the depot, and it's — well, kinda gross.

EARL: *standing*
Get to the point!

JACK:

Well — this story — I won't mention any names — has it there's a sweet little girl from the suburbs involved in some pretty funny business on the other side of town —

EARL: *impatient*
So?

JACK:

It's a real sideshow. You know — animal act — like the kinda stuff you were tellin' us *you* saw down in Vegas.

*He grins.*

Remember?

EARL:
> Yeah?

JACK:
> Yeah! Over on the other side a the river! I know you
> don't get into that part of town much, Mr. Jensen —
> lotta DP's, yuh know. Indians. But there's this big
> dumb bohunk over there who's got a *perfect* set-up —
> yuh know, bachelor pad, lotsa booze, the whole bit —

EARL:
> *And?*

JACK:
> And this sweet little chick from the suburbs gets the
> blocks put to her by the bohunk — every night, when
> her old man thinks she's at her pottery class!

EARL: *stunned*
> What?

JACK:
> So this story goes.

> *A pause.*

EARL:
> *Katharine?*

JACK: *hastily*
> No, Earl — *no*. It's just *gossip*, like I said. I only
> mentioned it because I thought maybe you should —
> put a stop to it —

EARL:
> It's a lie!

JACK:
> Sure — *I* know it's a lie. I wouldn't even a repeated it
> — but you gotta face facts. It's the kinda thing could
> ruin Kathy's reputation fer good.

EARL: *getting hold of himself*
Who — told you this?

JACK:
Let's see, I guess it musta bin Ricky. What was it the hippie said —? "Now she's used goods, man."

*EARL reacts to this.*

Course, nobody ever believes a thing he says anyway. Just a loudmouth — you know the kind. Always lookin' fer the worst in people.

EARL:
I'll put a stop to this nonsense right away.

*A pause.*

I appreciate it, Jack.

JACK:
Appreciate?

EARL:
Your — honesty. And, uh — one more thing. Who's the — culprit?

*A long pause.*

JACK:
Now, that's askin' a bit much, Earl. Don't forget I gotta *work* with these guys.

EARL:
*One of my drivers?*

JACK:
Well — I don't wanta get anybody in trouble. Maybe there's nuthin' to this. You see, in my position —

EARL:
> What's it worth to you?

JACK:
> I didden come here fer money, Earl.

EARL: *angrily*
> Well, what *did* you come for?

> *A pause. JACK shrugs.*

JACK: *smiling*
> The cost-a-livin' hike? Remember?

EARL: *pausing*
> Okay. Ten percent, across the board!

> *A pause.*

> And your usual commission.

JACK:
> I can't rat on a driver, Earl!

EARL:
> Who is it?

> *A pause. JACK looks pained.*

JACK:
> No, I just can't do it. Not to a buddy.

EARL:
> *Roychuk?* I'll —!

JACK:
> Hey, take it *easy*, Earl!

EARL:
I — I'll look after this now.

*In control.*

I can destroy this — rotten lie.

*A pause. EARL pours two drinks.*

Of course, none of this discussion will leave the office.

JACK:
Right you are, Earl.

*JACK salutes and drinks his whiskey.*

I'll, uh move along then.

EARL: *distantly*
Okay.

JACK: *going out*
And I'll bring that contract down next week! For your
John Henry.

EARL:
Yeah — sure. Sure.

*The instrumental music for "Earl's Aria" begins.*

EARL:
*Oh my God — not Kathy.*
*She's just a little girl!*
*She's still my baby daughter!*

JACK: *off*
*Now she's used goods, Earl.*

EARL:
>*All these drivers are like animals.*
>*They sneer about my wife.*
>*They've been lusting after Kathy*
>*And trying to wreck her life.*
>
>*My whole life's been a struggle*
>*To keep her sweet and pure.*
>*I did everything a father could*
>*And now it's spoiled for sure.*
>
>*I dreamed some day she'd marry*
>*An up-and-coming man.*
>*But now that's all been shattered.*

JACK: *off*
>*You gotta face facts, man.*

EARL: *angrily*
>*Well, it's my turn now for action.*
>*I'll find his crummy den.*
>*I'll have him beaten like a dog,*
>*And then —!*

>*EARL smashes the table with his glass. The*
>*music ends.*
>
>*JOHNNY and KATHY appear laughing and*
>*holding hands. KATHY's high spirits play off*
>*JOHNNY's nervousness as they approach the*
>*"door" of EARL's office.*

EARL:
>Katharine!

KATHY:
>Daddy, I have some *fantastic* news for you!

JOHNNY:
>Kathy! Would you just let me —?

KATHY:
>Oh, all right — he wants to tell you.

JOHNNY:
>I — we came — to ask you something, Earl. You see, Kathy and I have been — getting to know each other for a while and we — well, we thought it was time to come and talk about doing the right thing —

KATHY: *giggling at his embarrassment*
>Listen to him. Isn't he quaint?

EARL:
>Be quiet!

KATHY:
>Pardon?

EARL:
>Katharine — go inside while I deal with this — animal.

JOHNNY:
>Now, hang on, Earl. You're making a mistake.

EARL:
>When it's time to hear from you, I'll give your cage a shake!

KATHY: *confused*
>Daddy — what's *wrong*?

EARL:
>Will you go? This isn't for you to hear!

JOHNNY:
>Stay where you are, Kathy. You're old enough now.

EARL:
>*I'll* decide on her maturity, Roychuck! I make the decisions for *my* daughter! Not you!

JOHNNY:
    We already decided! *We* did! Kathy and me are
    getting married!

EARL:
    Married!

    *The instrumental music for "The Struggle Trio"*
    *begins.*

EARL:
    *What's wrong, Kathy, are you crazy?*
    *Is this respect for your family?*
    *I know his kind. They're all the same.*
    *To get your money he'll steal your name.*

KATHY:
    *Oh daddy, how can you say those things?*
    *We haven't rushed into this without a thought.*
    *There'll be all kinds of trials we have to face —*

JOHNNY:  *angrily*
    *Tell her what you mean, Jensen.*
    *Tell her how the bohunks beat their women.*
    *Go on! Tell her those worn-out lies again.*

EARL:
    *There! He said it himself. Did you hear him?*
    *They drink and fool and tear around,*
    *But the women sit home till they're old*
    *And worn right down.*
    *God, live with him,*
    *But don't get married!*
    *You think you're pretty smart, Roychuk.*
    *But you'll never drive a rig of mine again.*

JOHNNY:  *right back*
    *That's fine with me — Boss!*
    *You can take your truck and stick it!*
    to KATHY  *Come on! We're gettin' outta here!*

*JOHNNY moves toward the exit.*

KATHY:

> *Now just hold on — the two of you.*
> *Yelling and fighting won't get us through!*
> *Neither of you is being honest —*
> *Johnny, where's all that cool you promised?*
> *And daddy, you're being so unkind.*
> *Give him a chance to speak his mind.*
> *It must be the shock of finding out*
> *That your little girl is growing up.*
> *You've got to consider it while there's still time:*
> *I'm ready to be his, and he'll be mine.*

EARL:

> *No daughter of mine would marry his sort.*
> *They've all got a girl friend in every port.*

JOHNNY:

> *We made a big mistake coming here to you,*
> *We should'a just took off without even telling you.*
> *But I gotta do things straight and right —*
> *Not sneakin' round like a thief,*
> *In the middle of the night.*

EARL:

> *You listen to me, you worthless bum,*
> *It cost me a fortune to bring her up.*
> *She's used to having* everything *—*
> *Brand spanking new!*

KATHY:

> *Don't tell stories you know aren't true!*

JOHNNY:

> *I know what you're saying, tryna put me down.*
> *Okay, I come from the wrong side of town.*
> *But I learned early how to earn my own,*
> *And if you're talking about wild oats,*
> *They're already sown.*
> *I'm gonna marry her — I can treat her right.*
> *I didn't come here to start a fight.*

KATHY:

> *I know the kind of boy that you'd pick out*
> *But Johnny's the only man I'll ever love.*

EARL: *trying another tack*
> *Listen to me — you're both still kids.*
> *Let's forget about the things you did.*

JOHNNY AND KATHY:

> *We're not ashamed of what we're doing.*

EARL:

> *You'll forget all about him pretty soon.*

KATHY:

> *Now I'm old enough to live my own life.*

JOHNNY AND KATHY:

> *And with or without you,*
> *She (I'll) be my (his) wife.*

KATHY:

> *So please smile and wish us all the best.*
> *I know my Johnny'll take care of the rest.*

JOHNNY:

> *I can start my own business just like you.*
> *I've been driving long enough to know what I'm doin'.*
> *We'll build a home, and we'll get by.*

JOHNNY AND KATHY:

> *I will always be right by your side.*

EARL:

>Do you know what it is that hurts me most?
>The father is always the last to know.
>But I guess if you both really mean what you say —
>I won't be the one to stand in your way.

KATHY:

>Oh daddy, you're an angel! I love you so.

JOHNNY:

>Mr. Jensen, there's something you ought to know.
>We wouldn't have done it without your okay,
>'Cause I always did respect what you got to say.

EARL:

>Well, we'll have to start thinking in terms of you.
>Maybe there's a better job you can do.
>I'm not getting any younger as you can see.
>Someday you'll have to take over from me.
>It's a good chance for you to see what you got.
>Johnny, why don't you give it some thought?

KATHY:

>Everything's happening! It's just like a dream!

JOHNNY:

>The only thing that matters is you with me.

EARL:

>Kids these days are growing up too fast!

JOHNNY AND KATHY:

>Ours is a love that's going to last.

EARL:

>Well I'm sorry but I've got work to do.
>From here on in, it's up to you.

KATHY:

>I'll ask mother to start the plans.

JOHNNY:
>Sir, I'd like to shake your hand.

EARL:
>From now on John, it's dad — or Earl.

KATHY:
>Daddy, you've made me a happy girl!

>*At the end of the song, all three are standing together. The instrumental music for "The Wedding Song" begins. JOHNNY takes his place at the altar as the characters assemble in church for the wedding. EARL and KATHY march down the aisle.*

VOCAL CHORUS:
>*She's all in white. He's by her side.*
>*Today they're becoming man and wife.*
>*Choir begins to sing. He gives her the ring.*
>*She feels like a queen, and he's her king.*

>*The ceremony ends. KATHY and JOHNNY leave the church as the crowd, including JACK, FLORA, RICKY, EARL and the DANCERS, throws rice. They re-assemble for the wedding reception and dance. A bar is set up downstage.*

>*The instrumental music for "The Sugar Waltz" begins. EARL approaches KATHY and JOHNNY, downstage centre.*

EARL:
>Well. Am I entitled to the first dance?

JOHNNY:
>Sure — you go ahead — Dad.

>*They dance away to the right.*

But have her back before midnight!

*FLORA and JACK approach from the left.*

JACK:

Hey, good buddy! Can I buy a drink for the ole married man?

*He laughs.*

Sucker!

*JACK puts his arm around JOHNNY and takes him off to the bar at right leaving FLORA alone, downstairs centre. DEBBIE LOU and RICKY dance past.*

RICKY:
Hiya, Flora!

DEBBIE LOU:
How's tricks, Mrs. Deal?

FLORA:
Oh — Debbie. Don't tell me *you* got an invite!

DEBBIE LOU:
Johnny *said* I could come!

*ROY enters dressed up in new, but outrageous, clothes.*

ROY:

Hey, Flora! Wanna cut a rug?

FLORA:
Whudja, finish yer Arthur Murray course?

*ROY and FLORA dance off in real style. EARL and KATHY dance past.*

KATHY:
Daddy, I'm so happy, I could — explode!

EARL:
> Now Punkin, you shouldn't expect too much at first.

KATHY:
> Oh Father — *stop* it!

> *JOHNNY intercepts them from the right, a drink in his hand.*

JOHNNY:
> You don't mind if I cut in now, do you?

EARL:
> You're certainly impatient, I'll say that.

JOHNNY:
> Aa — it's just the ole "Ukrainian" in me — Dad.

> *He puts the drink in EARL's hand and dances off with KATHY. EARL goes to the bar, passing JACK, who meets RICKY and DEBBIE LOU dancing past. JACK cuts in.*

JACK: *to RICKY*
> Well, they really got this shindig organized in a hurry, didn't they? Didjuh see Earl's shotgun at the door?

> *He laughs.*

FLORA: *dancing past him*
> Oh shut up, Jack. Why don't yuh enjoy yourself for once?

> *RICKY cuts in on ROY as JACK and DEBBIE LOU dance off. FILTHY PHIL appears.*

FILTHY PHIL: *to ROY*
> Well, whuddayuh think? Bride looks a little plump around the middle of her wedding dress — eh?

ROY: *staring*
    Gowan!

> *FILTHY PHIL laughs and shoves ROY over toward the bar. KATHY and JOHNNY dance past.*

KATHY:
    What are you looking so scared for?

JOHNNY:
    The boys! I wonder if any of 'em found out where we're staying tonight?

KATHY: *feigning innocent curiosity*
    Why — was it supposed to be a secret?

> *JOHNNY looks around in horror. She smiles and hugs him. Suddenly, the Roychuck family enters dressed in traditional Ukrainian costume — the DANCERS.*

JOHNNY:
    Dobray Vetcheer!

> *Response.*

JACK: *to anyone*
    Roychuck's family's here! Kin smell the garlic from here!

JOHNNY:
    Hey — Kolomeyka!

> *The waltz ends.*

> *The dance floor clears as the "Kolomeyka" dance music begins. JOHNNY and KATHY are invited to participate and do. Gradually, all the DANCERS join in, led by RICKY who is enticed into the dance by a YOUNG WOMAN.*

JACK:

> Go on, hippie! Don't let 'em show yuh up!

KATHY:

> Try it out, Ricky!

DEBBIE LOU:

> If you dance with *her*, I'm goin' home with Scrotum!

> *The dancing builds to a display of wild rhythm*
> *accompanied by shouting and stomping. There*
> *is a great final shout and the stage suddenly*
> *goes black.*

# Act Two

*In the darkness, the instrumental music for "Cruel Tears" begins. The lights come up on the VOCAL CHORUS and on KATHY and JOHNNY in their home, Level 1. JOHNNY prepares to leave for work in the morning.*

VOCAL CHORUS:
> *A month goes by, that's not much time,*
> *But our couple's settled in just fine.*
> *Got a little suite just built for two*
> *In a modern block called the "Normanview."*
> > *Two years lease,*
> > *No pets, no kids.*   refrain   *No fun.*
> > *Right behind the shopping mall.*
> > refrain   *On the bus line.*
>
> *Johnny's a foreman, climbin' real fast.*
> *He wears a tie and his pants get pressed.*
> *Kathy's in the kitchen cookin' up a storm*
> *Sewin' all the curtains for their cozy little home.*
> > *Blind stitchin'!*

*JOHNNY leaves for work as KATHY bustles about in her "kitchen." The instrumental music for "The Catalogue Blues" begins. FLORA comes to the "door" and knocks.*

KATHY:
Hello?

FLORA:
Hiyuh.

KATHY:
Oh! Uh — Flora?

FLORA:
'At's right. We met at the wedding, remember?

KATHY:
Sure. You're uh — Jack's wife?

FLORA:
Yeah — Jack's wife.

*She laughs nervously.*

'At's me awright.

KATHY:
Come in, come in!

*A pause.*

How is — Jack?

FLORA:
Oh, real good. He always is.

KATHY:
I was uh, just putting the kettle on. Would you like some tea?

FLORA: *appalled*
>Tea?

KATHY:
>Oh, I have coffee too! It's only instant though. We haven't got our coffee-maker yet.

FLORA:
>No, no — tea's real good.

>*KATHY goes out to fill the kettle.*

KATHY: *from the "kitchen"*
>Would you like to try a cookie?

FLORA:
>A what?

KATHY:
>Oatmeal cookies! I'm learning a new recipe!

FLORA: *to herself, looking around*
>Oatmeal cookies. Frilly curtains in the kitchen. I'd forgot what it was like. Hmph. And all this new stuff.

>*KATHY returns.*

>Got a lotta nice things at the reception, eh?

KATHY:
>Yes — everybody was so generous! It was fantastic. And look!

>*She gets out an elaborately designed, expensive-looking neck scarf.*

>Johnny's mother gave me this beautiful scarf! Look at the *embroidery*!

FLORA:
> Yeah — real nice. Makes a difference when you get —
> personal things.

> *She hands it back.*

> Used the waffle iron yet?

KATHY: *confused*
> Waffle iron? Oh — yes!

> *She smiles.*

> Thanks very much. That was very — original.

FLORA:
> Yuh didden get no others, eh?

KATHY: *laughing*
> No! But we now have three toasters!

FLORA:
> Yeah, Jack 'n me got four electric can-openers at ours!

> *She laughs.*

> Well — as long as yuh got everythin' yuh need! Can't
> complain if it's free!

KATHY:
> Oh, we had to buy a *few* things — most of the big
> expensive ones.

FLORA:
> Well, I hope they last till yuh pay 'em all off.

KATHY:
> I beg your pardon?

FLORA:
> Our stuff fell apart before the first anniversary!
> Wherejuh get yours? Korman's Cut-Rate House of
> Bargains?

> *The VOCAL CHORUS sings "The Catalogue
> Blues."*

VOCAL CHORUS:
> *This year's hottest buy*
> *Is the deluxe range you'll need.*
> *Auto-cleaning oven, four oven racks,*
> *Self-basting rotisserie.*
> *With a camouflaged storage drawer*
> *To hide away all your pots and pans;*
> *Consul light, oven light,*
> *Illuminated broiler and*
> *A prismachrome, bastomatic roast meter*
> *To end those burnt supper blues.*
>
> *This five-cycle automatic washer*
> *Is the queen of versatility.*
> *Ten wash-spin speeds,*
> *Hot-cold water — selectivity!*
> *Heavy-duty agitator, lint-trap,*
> *With stop-action safety lid,*
> *Genuine imitation steel construction*
> *With plastic-coat front and sides,*
> *Porcelain-enamelled basket and top.*
>
> *Our finest quality dryer*
> *Along with the washer too*
> *Has automatic dry cycles normal*
> *And permanent press for you.*
> *No-heat cycle fluffs your towels.*
> *Safety stop switch, drum light.*
> *Comes in avocado, harvest gold,*
> *Ordinary beige and white,*
> *Mellow-tone green, little boy blue*
> *And deeeeep olive.*

refrain *Our couple can own some wonderful things*
*In just a year or two.*
*Once they've made the small down payment,*
*They're almost through.*

*How about a twenty-speed blender?*
*With eight push-button controls?*
*High-low selector switch,*
*Pulse-action works, with a durable plastic bowl.*
*Five-cup graduated glass container*
*And a one-ounce removeable top,*
*With electronic timer for split-second blending,*
*Also an automatic stop.*
*Removable blade assembly, and*
*At no cost to you, a full-colour cookbook!*

*Here's a honey of a buy, top of the line,*
*On a frost-free two-door fridge —*
*Good family size, lots of shelves*
*With trim along the ridge.*
*With a butter compartment and one for cheese,*
*And a big meat-keeper too,*
*Egg buckets, crisper,*
*And a freezer dispenser for your juice,*
*Charcoal filter, dual controls.*
*Limit of two per customer, please.*

*You absolutely need a brand new carvomatic*
*Slicelectric knife,*
*With stainless steel double-hollow-ground blades*
*That'll stay sharp all its life.*
*You'll get a push-button blade release*
*Complete with automatic stop.*
*Comes with exclusive wall rack table stand,*
*Set in a plastic chest*
*And a handy finger-tip on-off button,*
*Our ultimate in value, super-exclusive, this week only!*

refrain *You can own some wonderful things*
*In just a year or two.*
*Once you've made that small down payment —*
*You're almost through!*

FLORA:
> Yuh know, I just didden think you'd be the type to
> take up cookin' and cleaning and all that.

KATHY:
> Well — neither did I. Just *no way* Kathy Jensen was
> going to be trapped into a traditional housewife
> role —

FLORA:
> Now wait a minute!

KATHY: *laughing*
> Anyway, I *do* like cooking. Isn't that weird? I feel
> *great*, trying out new recipes. Making this place look
> like a home.

FLORA: *gazing at her*
> Uh huh.

> *A pause. The VOCAL CHORUS sings the refrain*
> *of "The Catalogue Blues."*

KATHY: *making conversation*
> Did you uh — walk over?

FLORA:
> No. No, I drove. Thought I'd be neighbourly and see
> how you're settlin' in tuh married life. Jack gimme
> the car today to get the groceries, so I dumped the
> kids off at Suzy's and —

KATHY:
> Oh, that's fan*tas*tic! You have kids!

FLORA:
Yeah — four of 'em.

KATHY:
Gee, you're lucky. Someday —!

FLORA:
Everyone of 'em an animal!

KATHY:
Oh.

*A pause.*

The water's boiling!

*KATHY goes to the "kitchen."*

FLORA: *calling*
So you really got yourself a prize, eh?

KATHY:
Pardon?

FLORA:
Johnny! I was sayin' he's some catch!

KATHY: *still in the "kitchen," making tea*
Well, I think he is!

FLORA: *to herself*
Half the wimmen in this town tried to snap him up!
Single *and* married. But he held out. "Lookin' fer
somethin' special," he sez. Just *like* a Uke.

*KATHY re-enters with the tea and some cups
and saucers.*

KATHY:
Sorry — what were you saying?

66

FLORA:
> Just pumpin' air, sweetie.

KATHY:
> What do you take?

FLORA: *automatically*
> Cream'n'sugar.

> *A pause.*

> Hey, tell me somethin'! Did you have some kinda plan, or what? Or was it *real love*? You know — stars fell on the Saskatchewan when I held you in my arms, eksetra, eksetra?

KATHY: *laughing*
> No, I think it just happened.

> *A pause.*

> Maybe it *was* the stars. He's a Leo, you know.

FLORA:
> He's a *what*?

KATHY:
> Leo — the lion? That's his sign.

> *The instrumental music for "The Homemaker's Duet" begins.*

FLORA: *ignoring KATHY's last line*
> Honey, you got any *idea* how many girls tried to trap up Johnny Roychuck?

KATHY:
> That's in the past, Flora! Sure — I know Johnny used to run around a lot, but we're married *now*. The past isn't important.

FLORA:
>I don't wanna disillusion yuh, kiddo, but it has a way of comin' back tuh haunt yuh, eh?

KATHY:
>Maybe that happens with other people, Flora.

FLORA: *laughing sharply*
>Yeah, maybe. But it's funny how long those old flames take to flicker out sometimes. Six months after Jack and me got married, he was comin' home from his road trips smellin' like cheap perfume.

KATHY: *uncomfortable*
>Well, I'm not saying married people don't have — problems. But I wouldn't have got married if Johnny wasn't really special.

FLORA:
>Everybody thinks *that*, sweetie-poo. One minute, you're standing up to your knees in rose petals, just dazzled by the godalmighty glory of it all!

KATHY:
>Yes!

FLORA:
>And the next, yer up to yer ass in dirty dishes and the old man's whining he doesn't have a clean shirt! To go out boozing with the boys!

KATHY: *turning away*
>Yeah — I suppose.

>*A pause.*

FLORA:
>Aw, I didden come over to ruin yer day. Maybe you *have* got it together. Who knows what we really want, eh?

*KATHY begins to sing "The Homemaker's Duet."*

KATHY:

> *Oh Flora, I'm so happy I got a good man.*
> *I couldn't ask for more.*
> *He's strong and yet he's gentle*
> *And he treats me like*
> *I've never been treated before.*
> *It might sound silly to talk this way,*
> *Like an empty-headed trucker's wife,*
> *But listen to me, Flora —*
> *I'm a woman,*
> *And there's a reason why I chose this life.*
>
> refrain *Living together with the one you love,*
> *Sharing all the work and play,*
> *Two people facing whatever comes along,*
> *Anticipating each new day.*

FLORA:

> *Lissen honey, just you wait,*
> *Let me tell you 'bout the life I've led.*
> *Waitin' fer that truckin' man of mine,*
> *Sleepin' in an empty bed,*
> *I bin talking to the radio lonely nights,*
> *Phoning up the Fifth Wheel Show,*
> *Knowin' he's livin' it up real high,*
> *Somewhere down the road.*
> *I'm wipin' runny noses, there's dirty diapers*
> *Soakin' in the biffy sink.*
> *It's an easy life for a trucker's wife,*
> *That's what I used to think.*
> *Our castle turned out to be a garbage dump,*
> *My hair is turnin' grey.*
> *It's a far cry from what he promised me*
> *On our weddin' day!*

refrain *Livin' together with the one yuh love,*
*Sharin' all the work and play.*
*Two people facin' whatever comes along,*
*Anticipatin' each new day!*

KATHY:
*I know it won't be an easy road,*
*It's full of twists and bends.*
*But Johnny and I are going down it,*
*Until we reach the end.*
*Maybe he's the driver but when I got married,*
*I learned how to read the maps.*
*I can be a housewife, but not some loser*
*Living in a laundromat.*

*A musical bridge.*

FLORA:
*Let me tell yuh, sweetie —*
*You don't know nothin' till yuh got four kids!*
*Sherry's got the measles, Mark'll be next,*
*And Angie's got a real boyfriend.*
*I'm run ragged from dawn to dusk*
*Picking up their odds and ends.*
*Jack drops in for a change of clothes,*
*He forgot about the times we had,*
*Baby Brent spends the whole day cryin'*
*And he looks just like his dad.*

FLORA AND KATHY:
refrain *Living together with the one you love*
*Sharing all the work and play.*
*Two people facing whatever comes along,*
*Anticipating each new day.*

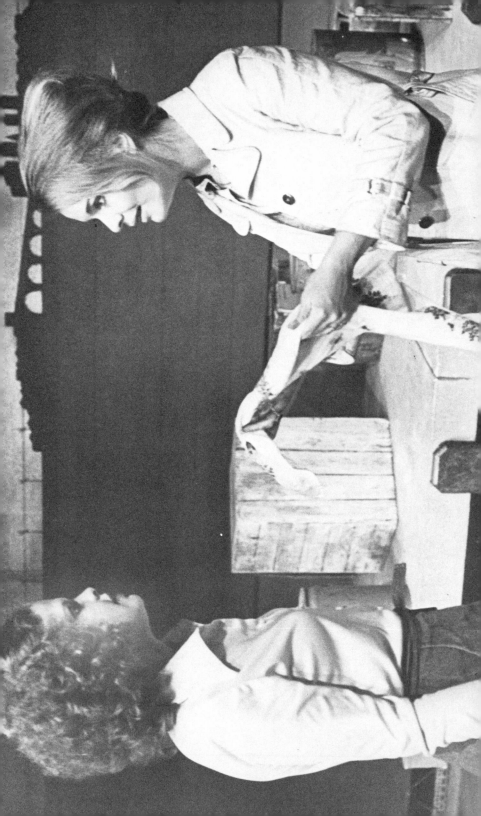

FLORA:
>*Pay no mind to what I say,*
>*I just been kicked around.*
>*Maybe it's true you'll have a good life,*
>*If your man keeps his feet on the ground.*
>*If he treats you right, the way he should,*
>*He'll always have your respect —*
>*And you'll always have colourful things*

>*A pause.*

*Like that scarf around your neck.*

>*The music continues instrumentally behind the*
>*dialogue. KATHY removes her scarf.*

KATHY:
Here. Take it, Flora — maybe it'll bring *you* some joy.

FLORA:
I can't! It's from Johnny's —

KATHY:
I want you to have it.

FLORA:
Won't he be — mad?

KATHY: *smiling*
He'd better not be! It's my scarf.

FLORA: *touched*
Thanks.

>*A pause.*

Well, I better go get the rations.

>*They go to the "door."*

KATHY:

I want you to come over any time you feel like it.
And bring your kids!

FLORA:

Yeah — you too. Now it's your turn to visit me.

KATHY:

Okay.

FLORA:

Just — gimme a call before yuh come over, eh?

*She goes.*

See yuh!

KATHY:

Bye-bye.

*The instrumental music for "The Loading Dock
Aria" begins. It is a simple percussion rhythm.
ROY, JACK and RICKY are loading a truck —
Roy's. At the other side, FILTHY PHIL and the
MALE NON-VOCAL CHORUS are loading a
truck with boxes. JACK stops work first.*

JACK:

*What're we doin' on the loadin' dock,
Liftin' heavy boxes till the boss says stop?
Johnny was our friend, but now he's on top
Watchin' us sweat on the loading dock!*

RICKY:

*We're workin' for the money.*

FILTHY PHIL:

*It ain't fer fun.*

ROY:

*We gotta do the work 'cause it's gotta be done.*

74

RICKY:
>  We're part of the company, according to John.

ROY:
>  Sweatin' for the money, not the fun.

RICKY:
>  We got plenty a muscle to make our way
>  If it's work by week or work by day.

FILTHY PHIL:
>  It don't matter too much when or where
>  If the pay is good and it's always there.

JACK:
>  This plan a his is a rip-off scheme!
>  It ain't as good as he makes it seem.
>  On an hourly rate we could featherbed;
>  Work by the mile and we're screwed instead!
>
>  Now if you listen to me, I got a plan.
>  Don't listen to Johnny, he's a company man.
>
>  Silence for one line.
>
>  Don't listen to Johnny, he's a company man.
>
>  RICKY and ROY stop work. The others continue.

RICKY:
>  Come on — we're all brothers. Johnny is too.

ROY:
>  He'll get us more bucks for what we're doin'.

JACK:

>*If you wanta slave go and dig ditches.*
>*Better'n makin' these bastards rich. If*
>*A man drives truck, he don't swing pick.*
>*An archy-tect won't lift no bricks.*
>*You guys run rigs, not garbage vans.*
>*A Knight of the Road is a driving man!*

>*As the second group continues to work,*
>*JOHNNY enters with a clipboard. He is*
>*surprised to see RICKY, ROY and JACK*
>*idling.*

JOHNNY:

What's up? Truck loaded awready?

JACK:

Naw, we took a little break.

JOHNNY: *checking his watch*

Little break? This ain't no government office, boys —
it's a truck depot! Now get movin', eh?

JACK: *to the others*

See what I say? Give a guy a bit of power and first
thing you know yuh got a little Hitler on your hands.

>*Laughter.*

JOHNNY:

Okay, you guys — cut the crap and get on with it.
This truck's due in Winnipeg by midnight. Roy, aren't
you supposeta be haulin' this?

ROY:

I'm just havin' a breather. All this liftin's gettin' us
down, Johnny. We ain't used to it.

JOHNNY:

Well, you better get used to it.

JACK:
> Hey, catch that, boys! Whatsa matter, big stud? Not gettin' enough from the ole lady?

JOHNNY: *bristling*
> What was that?

RICKY: *quickly*
> Hey Johnny! Payday today! How about comin' over to the Blacktop and drawin' a few with us! Like old times!

JOHNNY:
> I uh, don't think I can manage it today.

> *He concentrates on the clipboard.*

JACK:
> Old man Jensen keeps him on a short leash!

> *ROY laughs.*

JOHNNY:
> Well, if it's any a yer business, Kathy and me got something planned.

JACK:
> Well then — we'll just hafta carry on by ourselves, eh, boys? *Somebody's* gotta keep up the tradition.

RICKY:
> Couldenchuh drop by — fer a couple a quick ones? On your way home like?

ROY:
> Yeah — a couple a quick ones!

JOHNNY:
> I know what you guys mean. A couple a quick kegs!

JACK:
>Okay, buddy, you go home and crawl between the sheets. We wouldn't wanchuh to hit the boudoir polluted with . . .

>*Camping.*

>. . . "alcohol!"

JOHNNY: *laughing*
>You should talk! 'Member that night you were supposed to be home early for your anniversary dinner? I drank *you* right under the table!

>*They all laugh, including JACK.*

JACK:
>Yeah, that was a bash and a half!

>*He shakes his head.*

>Good times.

ROY:
>How 'bout it, Johnny? Gonna come and bite the head off a few weasels?

JOHNNY:
>Well — we'll see. Meantime, you guys get that pig *loaded*!

>*To ROY.*

>And I don't know why *you're* so eager! You're gonna be in Winnipeg tonight!

ROY:
>Aw, I'll get somebody to take my run — if yer gonna come ave a few wit' us. This is a real *celebration*!

JOHNNY:
>I'm not promisin' nuthin'! Now git those trucks looked after or we'll be here till this time tomorrow tryna do yesterday's work.

>>*The work rhythm begins again. JOHNNY goes out. JACK salutes him.*

>See you later — boss.

>>*The men laugh and chant the last stanza of the song.*

ALL THE TRUCKERS:
>*We got plenty a muscle to make our way*
>*If it's work by week, or work by day.*
>*It don't matter too much when or where*
>*If the pay is good and it's always there.*

>>*As they work, they move the boxes and props out and set up the scene for Jack's trailer. A raucous buzzer goes off. They drop everything and head out to the beer parlour as the lights go down.*

FILTHY PHIL:
>Hey — order me a rum! I gotta go drive my Mum home!

ROY: *to JACK*
>C'mon! Let's get Johnny!

>>*They exit.*

>>*In the darkness, the instrumental music for "Florazarea's Song" begins. The lights go up on FLORA, who is made up and looking prettier, in her trailer. She goes to the "phone" and dials.*

FLORA:

> Yeah, is Jack Deal there? Well, could you call him to
> the phone? I see. No, it's not important. He must be
> on the way now.

> *She hangs up.*

FLORA:

> *Oh, why do you treat me the way that you do?*
> *Why do you treat me this way?*
> *You're leaving me waiting while time goes along,*
> *Do you still love me today?*
>
> *I found you in the summertime,*
> *When the grass was green and the sun it shined,*
> *Now you're gone from these arms of mine.*
> *Oh why do you treat me this way?*
>
> *What went and happened to our yesterdays,*
> *Those days of laughter and wine?*
> *We treasured pressed roses and photographs*
> *Now crumpled and faded with time.*
>
> *We used to hold hands at the pitcher show,*
> *Kissing and watching our dreams unfold,*
> *But the screen went dark many years ago.*
> *Oh why do you treat me this way?*
>
> *You told me that first night you loved me*
> *And whispered you'd always be true,*
> *That maybe we'd have a few cloudy days*
> *But I could depend, darlin', on you.*
>
> spoken   *Then you started calling home "late from work.*
> *Around you I could hear all that beer parlour sound.*
> *I had to struggle to hold back my tears:*
> *"Okay sweetie, now don't let me down!"*

*Why did it have to turn out this way?*
*I'm so scared of bein' alone.*
*I've wasted my life away livin' this lie*
*And crying when you're never home.*

*I found you in the summertime*
*When the grass was green and the sun it shined,*
*Now you're gone from these arms of mine.*
*Oh, why do you treat me this way?*

> *A baby is heard crying, off. FLORA turns and exits. The music continues, but at a lower volume as JACK appears downstage left staggering drunkenly toward the door of his home. He is carrying a paper bag with a bottle in it. He stumbles into the trailer, cursing, and goes to the "radio," turning on the switch.*

JACK:   *calling*
Flora! Where are yuh?

> *The instrumental music shifts to a fast version of "Florazarea's Song," very loud. FLORA re-enters hastily and turns down the volume. It will gradually rise again through this scene.*

FLORA:
Will you shut up? I just got the kids tuh bed.

·JACK:
Lissen, getcher self fixed up. There's people on their way over here!

FLORA:
What?

JACK:
I invited the boys over for a little party!

FLORA:
Over *here*?

JACK:

Yeah! We haven't had a Friday night whingding fer a *long* time!

FLORA:

Oh shit!

JACK:

Come on, *hustle* will yuh? They're gonna be here any minute! Just went home to collect the wimmen.

FLORA:

Well, call 'em up and tell 'em the whole thing's off. I'm not up to no party tonight.

JACK:

Hey, don't be an ole granny now! You're always bitchin' that we never do nothing or see nobody!

FLORA:

Well, there's such a thing as lettin' me know when —

JACK:

Okay, I'll call it off! Just don't come whining tuh me the next time yer feelin' "lonely!"

FLORA:

Well, if that doesn't take the goddamn cake! I had to carry all the groceries in here by *myself*! *After* I took the car into the garage!

JACK:

What?

FLORA:

The clutch fell outtuv it again!

JACK:

*Wimmen drivers!* I don't know why I even let you drive it!

FLORA:

Cuz if you didn't, you'd hafta do all the errands yourself.

JACK:

*Oh yeah?*

FLORA:

Then you woulden have time to tear around, gettin' hammered up and chasin' wimmen in the beer parlours! Why do you bother even comin' home?

JACK:

Good question! Maybe cuz I was dumb enough tuh *marry* yuh!

FLORA:

Well, you didn't have to ask.

JACK:

I never asked! I was told!

FLORA:

Well, what was *I* supposeta do? Have the kid in a granary?

JACK:

Maybe yuh should've. Then yuh wouldn't be *bitchin'* about it alla time!

FLORA:

*Me* bitching? You're never here to listen! If I ever got started on all the things that —!

JACK:

Well, *don't* start! Get this damn trailer cleaned up so my friends don't think we live in a pig-sty!

> *The music has reached a peak in volume and FLORA turns down the "radio." The music goes quiet again.*

FLORA:
You clean it up! It's you wants the party.

JACK: *dangerously*
You're gonna make me do something both of us are gonna be sorry for.

FLORA:
You can't scare me with that kinda hard talk. Not with all yer friends comin' over. Don't want 'em to get all upset at the sight of blood — *do* we?

*The music ends. One of the VOCAL CHORUS breaks in like a radio announcer.*

VOCAL CHORUS:
Temperature in downtown Saskatoon a balmy seventy-eight degrees. *And* here's a new cut off the latest album from *The Dumptrucks!*

*The instrumental music to "Florazarea's Song," slow version, begins.*

*JACK pours himself a drink.*

JACK:
Roychuck's comin' over.

FLORA:
Johnny?

JACK:
Yeah — thought that'd cheer yuh up.

FLORA:
Is — Kathy comin' too?

JACK:
He says she is. Went home to get her anyways.

*He laughs.*

FLORA:
What's so funny?

JACK:

I'd like to see the look on her face, when he gets home!

FLORA:
Why?

JACK:

Aw — him and Ricky got involved in a little chug-a-lug contest!

*He laughs again.*

They're both half-pissed!

FLORA:
Tryna start trouble awready?

JACK:

Hell, no! Just tryna show him what he got himself in for!

FLORA:
I hope they come.

JACK:

Aaa — forget it. She isn't gonna lower herself to take in a truck driver party! He'll hafta knock some sense into her first.

FLORA:
You don't know anything about her!

JACK:

Izzat so? Well, what would I *want* to know?

FLORA: *pausing*
>It wouldn't make any difference. You gonna gimme a hand to clean this up?

JACK: *giving her a kiss*
>Lissen, I gotta take a shower! Armpits smell like a farmer's socks!

FLORA: *protesting*
>Well, look at this place. It'll take at least an hour!

JACK:
>Aa, do whutchuh can.

>*He notices the scarf around her neck that KATHY gave her.*

>Hey, wherejuh get that?

FLORA: *pausing*
>I bought it.

JACK:
>To hell you did! You can't afford *that* kinda silk!

>*He seizes the scarf.*

>Where'd you get it?

FLORA:
>A friend give it to me.

>*He twists the scarf.*

JACK:
>Friend? What friend? The milkman? Or you started takin' *hippies* in off the street?

FLORA: *choking*
>Kathy.

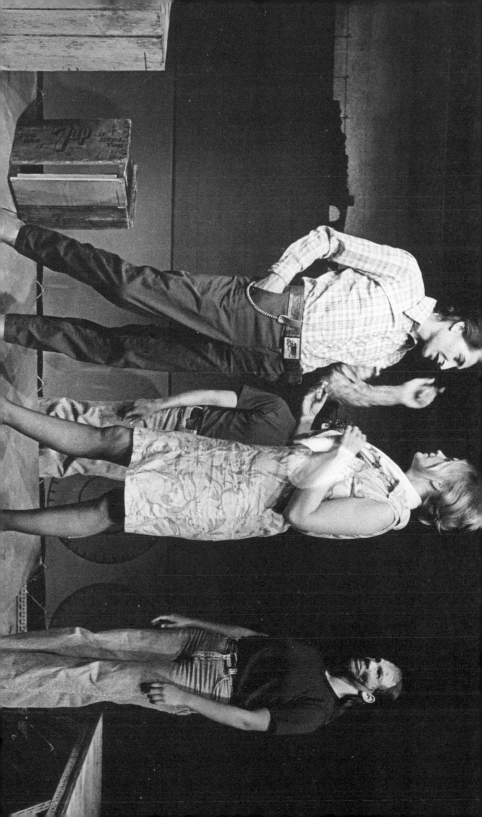

JACK:
> You're lyin'. She don't know *you!*

FLORA:
> I went over to visit her.

JACK:
> And she *donated* you a fifty dollar scarf? Just like that?

FLORA:
> Yes.

JACK:
> Who's she think she is — the Salvation Army?

FLORA:
> She didn't need it.

JACK:
> Neither do you. So you can hand it right back.

FLORA:
> I could wear it tonight.

JACK:
> Like hell you can. Think I want my wife wearing cast-offs — like some welfare bum? Take it off!

FLORA:
> No.

JACK: *shouting at her in a fury*
> *You take it off!*

> > *He tears the scarf from her throat, throwing her to the floor. The lights go up on the downstage area as ROY and DEBBIE LOU enter. ROY is carrying a case of beer. JACK exits through the rear.*

ROY:
> Hey, juh hear that?

DEBBIE LOU:
> What?

> *They listen.*

ROY:
> Jack and Flora — havin' another lovers' quarrel.

DEBBIE LOU:
> Gee, maybe the party's off.

ROY:
> Naaa — give 'em a minute tuh cool down.

> *A pause.*

> Like a beer? Sorta nice out here, izzen it?

DEBBIE LOU:
> Yeah — giss so.

> *ROY opens the case of beer. He uncaps two bottles with his teeth and hands one to DEBBIE LOU.*

ROY:
> Wanna go and sit down over by them lilacs?

DEBBIE LOU:
> Lissen, dummy — you said "a ride to the party."
> I don't wanchuh droolin' all over my dress again.

ROY:
> Awww!

DEBBIE LOU:
> *You* go over by the lilacs!

*ROY goes over to pee. The instrumental music
for "Roy's Aria" begins.*

ROY:

*I can see you standing
In your satin evening gown.
You'll dance with all the fellas here
But you just put me down.
I'm good, I'm bad, I have my faults,
I'm just like all the rest —
But still you make me feel that
I am less than second best.*

*When I come a-callin',
You're never there at home.
There's a light up in your window,
And I'm standin' here alone.
But when you never answer
It hurts me I confess.
Still you make me feel that
I am less than second best.*

*When they play the last waltz
And all the lovers dance,
I'll come up and ask you
But I won't stand a chance.
I know you'll laugh and turn away
And think I'm just a pest.
Still you make me feel that
I am less than second best.*

*Still you make me feel that
I am less than second best.*

*DEBBIE LOU replies, singing "Liberated Lady."*

DEBBIE LOU:

> *I know you see me every night*
> *Slingin' trays of foam,*
> *The boys all grabbin' at my butt*
> *And tryna get me home.*
>
> *But when the lights flick off and on*
> *And it's time to think of bed,*
> *I want a dude*
> *That isn't rude*
> *To spread butter on my bread.*
>
> refrain *I'm a liberated lady*
> *And I'll just wait and see.*
> *I got a lotta Friday nights*
> *To get what's in store for me.*
>
> *To love some mother's darlin'*
> *You'll spend your life alone*
> *Waitin' for that Romeo*
> *To ring your telephone.*
>
> *An instrumental break.*
>
> *They tell me that I'm burnin' out*
> *My candle from both ends.*
> *I'm old enough to know better*
> *But young enough to do it again.*
>
> *No one claims this heart of mine,*
> *Nobody owns my soul.*
> *Life is short,*
> *So come on, sport,*
> *And let those hot dice roll!*
>
> refrain *I'm a liberated lady*
> *And I'll just wait and see.*
> *I got a lotta Friday nights*
> *To get what's in store for me.*

*RICKY, FILTHY PHIL and the FEMALE NON-*
*VOCAL CHORUS enter carrying more beer.*

RICKY: *drunk*
>Hey, zis where the party is?

DEBBIE LOU:
>Yeah, you're here! Roy's over waterin' the lawn!

FILTHY PHIL:
>Hey Jack! We're comin' in, ready or not!

DEBBIE LOU:
>Party! We're gonna have a party!

RICKY: *pounding at the door*
>*Heeyy!* Any stompers at this soiray?

ROY:
>Jack! We're here!

>*FLORA opens the "door."*

FLORA:
>Will you guys shut up? You'll wake up the whole
>trailer court!

DEBBIE LOU:
>Hi Flora.

>*Going in.*

>Not puttin' yuh to any trouble, are we?

FLORA:
>Well, don't let it get you down, Chastity.

ROY: *going in*
>Where'za bar, Flora?

FILTHY PHIL: *crowding in behind with the girls*
Hi Flora! Hey, let's have some music!

DEBBIE LOU: *to ROY*
Whudjuh bring, dummy?

ROY:

Whud I *bring*? Kar-Tel's Fifty Greatest *Hit*!

*He takes out his record and puts it on the
"record player." They all freeze, listening.*

VOCAL CHORUS:
*This is the shortest song in the world.*

*JACK enters, dressed up.*

FILTHY PHIL:
Hey, where's your handbag?

JACK:

I was gittin' worried you guys weren't gonna show.
Crack me a beer, will yuh hippie?

*RICKY opens JACK a beer.*

What sorta music yuh gonna give us tonight, dumbell?

ROY:
All the golden oldens!

*Freeze.*

VOCAL CHORUS:
*Moose Jaw, Plunkett, Pile of Bones,
Amazon, Climax, Yellowgrass.
Zelma, Zenon Park, Goin' Home,
Saskatoon, Elbow, Gopherzazz!*

JACK:
Where's alla potato chips and stuff, Flora?

94

FLORA:
>You'll hafta go down to the store and get it!

JACK:
>Who's gonna entertain our guests? Jeez, somebody's gotta look after things.

>*FLORA shrugs and leaves.*

>And while yer out, pick up a couple a six-packs!

>*Freeze.*

VOCAL CHORUS:
>*Bacon for people who like their eggs fried greasy,*
>*Glass of milk and a coffee to go.*
>*Who's got time for a meal, when you're cooking up a deal?*
>*You got the runs on the road.*

JACK;
>Who'd you come with tonight, Debbie Lou?

DEBBIE LOU:
>Oh, nobody special — Roy gimme a ride over.

JACK: *putting his arm around her*
>Don't go away, I got somethin' to show you later on.

DEBBIE LOU:
>Well, I hope it's bigger'n last time!

>*Freeze.*

VOCAL CHORUS:
>*Keep your hands to yourself*
>*'Cause what I got is mine, all mine.*
>*Keep your hands in your pockets,*
>*'Cause what you want is mine, all mine.*

FILTHY PHIL:
>Hey Roy! Yer old flame's comin' over tonight!

ROY:
>Who?

FILTHY PHIL:
>Kathy Jensen! I mean, Roychuck.

ROY:
>Yeah — remember when she was a little kid, she used
>to ride her bike out to the depot?

>*To the others.*

>Filthy Phil always stayed late, so's he could watch
>her climb off in her skirt!

>*They all laugh. Freeze.*

VOCAL CHORUS:
>*I'm just a moan-in' moan-in' over you.*
>*Just a moan-in' moan-in' over you.*
>*Why can't you be true? Be true? Be true? Be true?*

ROY:
>Hey — my record!

JACK:
>Dammit, Ricky, if you can't stand up, get away from
>the stereo!

DEBBIE LOU:
>Anybody know if Johnny's comin' over?

FILTHY PHIL:
>S'pose to. Why?

DEBBIE LOU:
>I dunno, just like to see him again.

FILTHY PHIL:
>Look at her — gonna pine away!

RICKY:
> Forget him, Debbie Lou! *I'll always* love yuh!

> *Freeze.*

VOCAL CHORUS:
> *Don't push that button 'less you mean it,*
> *Or you're in for the shock of your life!*
> *Well, the sign said "Danger," but I couldn't read it,*
> *'Cause I left my bifocals at home.*

>> *During the previous exchange, FILTHY PHIL*
>> *has been preparing his coat-hanger trick which*
>> *is to fasten a coat hanger to ROY's belt, cover*
>> *it with a towel, then urge him to stand up.*

DEBBIE LOU: *pleased with the trick*
> Oh, you dirty thing!

JACK: *laughing*
> Know what, Roy? Kathy told me at the wedding she
> was really disappointed in you.

ROY:
> Huh? Why?

JACK:
> Said if you'd come onto her like a big stud — she
> wouldn't a married the Yewkeranian!

ROY:
> G'wan!

JACK:
> It's true! She had a crush on you for *years*. And yuh
> never gave her *nuthin'*.

ROY:
> G'wan!

*JACK whips the towel off the coat-hanger,*
*laughing uproariously.*

JACK:

Din't know you never *had* nuthin'!

*Freeze.*

VOCAL CHORUS:

*Ne pas actionez la chaise*
*Quand le train est en gare.*
*Don't tell me that*
*You just don't care.*

RICKY:

Hey, don' start buggin' *Roy*, or he'll end up doin'
somethin' crazy again.

JACK:

Who cares?

RICKY:

I care! He shouldn't be scarin' hell outta Katy! She
isn't the kinda chick you're useta boogyin' around
with.

JACK: *pausing*

Oh? Somethin' special, is she? You sayin' she's
better'n our bohunk friend deserves?

RICKY:

I d'int say that!

*JACK takes out a mickey of rye.*

JACK:

Yer slurring your words. Better have a drink.

*Freeze.*

VOCAL CHORUS:
>*Because I'm drinking more and enjoying it less,*
>*Since you walked out on me — baby.*

*JACK takes RICKY to one side.*

JACK:
>I been thinkin', Rick. How did a great guy like
>Johnny get mixed up with — Kathy Jensen?

RICKY:
>Yeah, lucky bugger! I coulden get to firs' base with
>her.

JACK:
>Aa, but she's a stuck-up bitch. Be just like every other
>broad in a year.

RICKY:
>Not her — too much class.

JACK:
>Well, she'll be sorry she married a Knight of the
>Road. You know what a chick like her needs?
>Somebody really, you know, *far out.*

RICKY: *laughing*
>Like you?

JACK: *pausing*
>So you used to be kinda sweet on her, eh, Rick? Have
>another shot of rye.

*He pours him a drink. Freeze.*

VOCAL CHORUS:
>*Just give me one more drink*
>*Of good old number one —*
>*Then you can carry me home.*

ROY:

Hey Debbie, you wanna go and check out Jack's bedroom?

DEBBIE LOU:

What for, fer cryin' out loud?

ROY:

He might have some gin stashed in there! Wanna go look?

DEBBIE LOU:

You dummy! Think I'd fall for that one?

FILTHY PHIL:

How about *this* one?

*He gooses her. Freeze.*

VOCAL CHORUS:

*She had long red hair
Streamin' down her back.
None on her head,
Just on her back!*

RICKY:

So — what're yuh tellin' me all this for?

JACK:

Well, I was talkin' to sweet little Kathy at the wedding, Rick. She's still stuck on yuh, buddy. Didjuh know that?

RICKY:

What?

JACK:

You know — on your wave length? In fact, she passed on this scarf of hers.

*JACK takes out KATHY's scarf which he has had in his pocket.*

RICKY:
Whaaah?

JACK:
Beautiful, isn't it?

*RICKY takes the scarf and fondles it.*

RICKY:
Jus — like — her.

JACK:
Just like her.

*Freeze.*

VOCAL CHORUS:
*I don't stand a chance*
*If I don't know the dance.*
*I didn't come all the way to Calgary,*
*Just to see you with another man.*

*The lights come up on JOHNNY and KATHY who are near the trailer, apparently arguing. FLORA enters with the groceries and the beer. The instrumental music for "The Party Boogie" quietly begins.*

FLORA:
Hi, you guys!

*She goes to JOHNNY and KATHY.*

What're you doin' out *here*?

KATHY:  *at the same time as JOHNNY*
Looking for something.

JOHNNY: *at the same time as KATHY*
>Just got here.

FLORA:
>Hey! You two fightin' awready?

KATHY AND JOHNNY:
>Nooo!

FLORA:
>I kin always tell. Come on, what happened?

KATHY:
>Flora, it's so damn — silly —

JOHNNY:
>It's *nuthin'*. Guess I was a little late gettin' home from the Blacktop —

KATHY:
>I didn't mind you being late — if you'd just *called* —

FLORA:
>Aaa — that's nothin' to fight about! Ferget about it! Come on in and have a good time!

>>*FLORA enters the trailer with KATHY and JOHNNY. "The Party Boogie" instrumental music comes up loud. Everybody dances enthusiastically.*

>Look who I found outside waitin' fer an invitation!

ROY:
>Hey, Johnny's here!

JACK:
>And *Mrs.* Roychuck!

*The crowd greets them lustily. RICKY, at a gesture from JACK, jams the scarf into his pocket.*

JOHNNY:
Hi, ever'body!

KATHY:
Hello.

JACK:
Okay — now we're all set to *boogie!*

*Freeze on gestures of drinking, dancing, feeling, with JACK overseeing it all.*

VOCAL CHORUS:
*Everybody's gonna have a real good time
Knocking back the beer, chugging five star rye,
Dancing up a storm to the stereo!
You gotta watch out boy, or you'll let it go.*

*This is no ordinary pay-cheque spree,
Drinkin' all night, coppin' feels for free.
Things are goin' on that you just don't see;
There's gonna be trouble! Jack's the key!*

*The instrumental music continues. JACK leads JOHNNY to the exit step of the trailer, ostensibly to give him a drink. KATHY is left alone. FLORA goes toward her, but RICKY arrives there first. He is drunk.*

RICKY:
H'ya, Kathy!

KATHY:
Hi, Ricky. Long time, no see.

RICKY:
Howya bin doin'?

KATHY:
Oh — okay.

RICKY:
Hey, you wanna dance?

*KATHY looks around for JOHNNY.*

KATHY:
Well uh — sure. I'd love to.

*There is no room to dance in the trailer so RICKY takes her outside past JACK and JOHNNY. RICKY and KATHY begin dancing in a way which indicates that they have danced before. RICKY becomes quite lewd. KATHY thinks he is clowning and laughs at the joke.*

JACK:
Kathy sure does a mean two-step, don't she?

JOHNNY: *sourly*
Yeah, so it seems.

JACK:
She's a real nice chick, Johnny.

*RICKY makes a suggestive gesture.*

JOHNNY:
Yeah.

JACK:
Aaa — don't worry about that! Ricky isn't gonna do nuthin' outta line. Had a few too many!

JOHNNY:
He never could hold his liquor.

JACK: *calling to KATHY and RICKY*
Hey, you two! Don't get all hot and bothered. This ain't a cathouse!

*He laughs.*

Guess he don't realize you're the boss now, eh, Johnny?

JOHNNY:
What's that got to do with anything?

JACK:
Well — yer his *supervisor.*

JOHNNY:
You don't have to be a supervisor to straighten Ricky out.

JACK:
That's for damned sure! But Ricky doesn't need straightenin' out. He's a good driver!

JOHNNY: *snarling*
Is that a fact?

JACK:
Hey, take it easy. I didden say *nuthin'!*

JOHNNY:
He's a back-door creeper! You gotta watch his kind.

JACK:
Ricky? Naaa.

*A pause.*

Oh you mean, when they useta go to high school together, they, uh — you know?

*JOHNNY shrugs.*

Hey, *careful*, John . . .

*JOHNNY rises violently.*

Now, take it easy, ole buddy. We're all friends here
tonight. Knights of the Road — remember?

JOHNNY: *ominously*
Kathy!

*KATHY and RICKY don't hear.*

Katharine!

KATHY: *laughing*
Sorrrrry! Card's full. You'll have to wait till the next
dance!

JOHNNY:
That's enough.

KATHY:
Can't hear yoooooo!

JOHNNY: *shouting at her*
Stop dancing!

*The music stops abruptly. The crowd moves
outside. KATHY moves anxiously toward
JOHNNY.*

KATHY:
Johnny?

RICKY:
Hey, where yuh goin'? Arnchuh gonna finishuh dance?

JOHNNY:
Finish it yourself, loverboy!

RICKY:
Whatsat supposetuh mean?

JOHNNY:
It means you got trouble if you don't start walkin'!

RICKY:
"J.R." speaks!

JACK:
Okay boys — we don't want any trouble!

JOHNNY:
There isn't gonna be no trouble.

JACK:
There's other ways of settlin' fights, yuh know.

KATHY: *upset*
They're not fighting! Listen, Johnny — we were *dancing* — there's nothing to be ashamed —

JOHNNY: *cutting her off, speaking to RICKY*
I hear yer turnin' into a hot shot driver.

RICKY:
I'm makin' my way!

JOHNNY:
And now yer goin' around braggin' about bein' the top driver in the company!

RICKY: *grinning*
Can't disappoint the ladies, "J.R."

JOHNNY:
Think yer good enough to beat my time on a run to Edmonton?

RICKY:
Chrise, pick a tuffy! I beat that one months ago!

JACK:
>Now don't get all *serious* about this, you guys. You
>need somethin' you kin settle right *now*!

KATHY:
>Johnny, don't you do anything silly!

JOHNNY:
>Canchuh see? He's just *beggin'* fer a lickin'!

KATHY:
>Johnny!

JACK:
>Whuchuh say, hippie, gonna take that?

KATHY:  *terrified*
>Johnny — let's go home *now*!

RICKY:  *back-pedalling*
>I don't wanta fight yuh, Johnny.

JOHNNY:
>I'll tell you what, hotshot! You got your car outside?
>Any distance you want! Start from the front door for
>our cars, and the first guy back wins.

JACK:
>Right! And the loser quits the company?

>*The crowd reacts.*

RICKY:
>Soun's fair! Less go!

KATHY:
>Please don't, Johnny!

JACK:
>Okay, here's yer route! Out the freeway to Number
>Eleven, around the cloverleaf and back here to the
>front door!

FLORA:
>Jack, you better stay outta this.

JOHNNY:
>First one back to the party, right?

RICKY:
>Have a beer ready for me!

KATHY:
>Johnny, I won't let you!

JOHNNY:
>Let *go* of me, will yuh?

KATHY:
>If you get into that car, I'm walking home!

>*JOHNNY hesitates.*

RICKY:   *nearly unconscious*
>C'mon, quit stallin', *boss*!

>*He staggers and nearly falls.*

FLORA:
>Jack, you gotta stop this! Ricky's stoned outtuv his
>mind.

ROY:
>Naw, he's okay.

RICKY:
>Surrr! I'm okay!

JACK:
>Atsa spirit, hippie! Now, yuh both know where yer goin'?

KATHY:
>Johnny, I warned you!

JOHNNY: *snarling at her*
>Yeah, yuh warned me. Now get inside and *shut up*!

>>*He pushes her roughly aside. She retreats offstage in slow motion. The instrumental music for "The Race Ballad" begins. JOHNNY and RICKY step to their cars in duel-like slow motion. The lights fade to black.*

JACK:
>On your marks! Get set! GOOOOO!

ROY:
>Come on, hippie — lay rubber!

FILTHY PHIL:
>Get that Barracuda movin', yuh big hunky!

>>*The lights come up on the VOCAL CHORUS. They sing "The Race Ballad." There are special lighting effects on JOHNNY and RICKY and on the singer in the VOCAL CHORUS who is singing "The Race Ballad."*

VOCAL CHORUS:
>*Now all you blacktop truckers,*
>*Who think you know the road:*
>*Be wary of the bottle*
>*'Cause it can take control.*
>*With whiskey, hate and stupid pride*
>*A mixture to avoid,*
>*The tale we'll tell is all of this,*
>*So listen closely boys.*

116

*The folly of a reckless man*
*Is very plain to see;*
*A test of manhood from the glass*
*Will end in misery.*
*Will surely end in misery.*

*It started at a party,*
*A crazy drunken spree.*
*Ricky had his foolish pride*
*And Johnny, jealousy.*
*Ricky said to Johnny,*
*"I'm just as good as you!"*
*Johnny said, "You son of a bitch,*
*I'll prove that isn't true."*

*They run outside blind with rage*
*And start up their machines.*
*The night is dark, but stars blaze down*
*Upon this frantic scene.*
*Tires just a-screamin',*
*They take off on their ride,*
*And hit the freeway flyin',*
*Wild fever in their eyes.*

*The 'cuda hits the Ruth Street ramp,*
*Huggin' to the line.*
*Ricky with his Charger floored*
*Isn't far behind.*
*By Preston they are neck and neck,*
*Blood rushing through their veins,*
*But the cloverleaf is comin' fast,*
*Just a single lane.*

*Ricky puts it to the mats,*
*He's doin' ninety-five.*
*The exit sign says twenty per;*
*Can he take the turn alive?*
*He hits the inside shoulder,*
*Goes fishin' round the curve,*
*Johnny hard upon his tail,*
*Straining every nerve.*

*They take off from the Eighth Street curve,*
*Burning up the night,*
*The city centre ramp appears,*
*Glaring in their lights.*
*Squealing through the cloverleaf,*
*Heading back to town,*
*Johnny edging closer,*
*Tryin' to shut him down!*

*Back along the freeway,*
*They're locked in overdrive.*
*Fighting for position,*
*Holding side by side,*
*Rick looks out his window,*
*Sees Johnny's face all white.*
*All Johnny sees is Kathy's face,*
*Ghost-like in the night.*

*Nearly at the finish ramp,*
*Ricky shoots ahead,*
*But this time his number's up,*
*The curve beats him instead.*
*Johnny sees the Charger*
*Go spinning through the air,*

    *Slowing down.*

*Burning, twisting, crazy,*
*Like a pinwheel at the fair.*

    *There is a shattering explosion of metal and*
    *glass or a stylized musical effect such as a*
    *broken string. The lights fade slowly on the*
    *VOCAL CHORUS as they sing the song's*
    *refrain.*

*The folly of a reckless man*
*Is very plain to see;*
*A test of manhood from the glass*
*Will end in misery.*
*Will surely end in misery.*

*The stages goes black.*

# Act Three

*Darkness. The sound of wind blowing is heard.*
*The instrumental music for "Lady Two" begins*
*as the lights come up very dimly to reveal*
*RICKY lying face down, lower left and*
*JOHNNY wandering around in the darkness.*

JOHNNY:
    Ricky! Where are you? *Ricky!*

RICKY: *moaning*
    Ohhhh!

*JOHNNY goes to RICKY.*

JOHNNY:
    Hey, come on, buddy! You're okay. You can't fool
    me!

RICKY:
    Ohhhhh . . .

JOHNNY:
> See — you're okay!

> *He forces a laugh.*

> Come on, get some life into yuh! Crowd's gonna be here any minute!

> *RICKY coughs painfully.*

> Okay, yuh just got the wind knocked outta yuh. Sit up now.

> *He helps RICKY sit up.*

> Is that better?

RICKY:
> Uhhhh.

JOHNNY:
> Okay, now stand. Attaboy. Startin' tuh come back to you now?

RICKY:
> Yeah . . .

JOHNNY:
> Man, the way you came off that ramp!

> *He laughs.*

> Looked like Awful Knawful jumpin' Blackstrap Canyon!

> *RICKY laughs painfully.*

RICKY:
> Boy, we sure do some crazy things!

JOHNNY:
>Okay, don't worry. It's all over and done with.

RICKY: *still dazed, shaking his head*
>Like idiots!

JOHNNY:
>Here comes the party. Got it together?

RICKY:
>I remember! You thought I was — messing around — with Kathy.

>*A pause.*

JOHNNY:
>Awright — forget it!

>*ROY runs in with JACK and DEBBIE LOU.*

ROY: *surveying the wreckage*
>Holy Hannah!

RICKY: *grinning*
>I pulled out to pass th' ramp!

JACK:
>That car is *lunched*!

JOHNNY:
>Don't worry. We got it all looked after.

JACK:
>Cops are on the way. Looks like Ricky's got some explainin' to do.

JOHNNY:
>I said it's under control.

>*Sirens begin, off.*

RICKY:

> You don't hafta get mixed up in this, Johnny. It's my car. I can take the rap.

JOHNNY:

> You keep quiet and do exactly what I tell you.

RICKY:

> Whuddayuh mean?

JACK:

> He said — keep your mouth shut!

JOHNNY:

> I'm the supervisor! I can handle the cops.

RICKY: *angrily*

> Lissen, this isn't your hassle!

JOHNNY:

> Like hell it isn't! I'm responsible for the company — and if the paper hears about this, it means bad P.R.

RICKY:

> Bad *P.R.*! For the *company*!

JOHNNY:

> Now relax and let me take care of it.

ROY:

> I hope you got a good story, Johnny. That car looks like it drove through a rolling mill.

JOHNNY: *to RICKY*

> You got blood on your face. Better get it wiped off.

> *RICKY, glaring resentfully, takes out KATHY's scarf and begins to wipe his face.*

RICKY:

> Zat got it?

124

JOHNNY:
>What's that?

RICKY: *startled*
>What?

JOHNNY: *advancing*
>Where'd you get that scarf?

RICKY: *staring at the scarf*
>Well — it's just an old piece of —

>*He realizes whose scarf it is and tries to hide it.*

JOHNNY:
>Let — me — see it!

ROY:
>Hey, what's goin' on?

DEBBIE LOU:
>What's happenin'?

RICKY:
>Johnny, lissen — it doesn't mean anything —

JOHNNY:
>I want that —

RICKY:
>She didn't —

JOHNNY:
>— scarf —

RICKY:
>— do nuthin' —

JOHNNY:
>— *now!*

RICKY:
>Hey!

>*They fight. JOHNNY punches RICKY to the ground, then begins kicking him in a frenzy.*

JOHNNY:
>You sneaking — lying — bastard!

ROY:
>Johnny, cool it!

JACK:
>Grab him! He's flippin' out!

DEBBIE LOU:
>Stop it, you guys!

ROY:
>Cops are comin'!

>*JOHNNY is subdued. A COP appears.*

COP:
>Okay — what's going on here?

JACK:
>Nothing.

ROY:
>Little — accident.

COP:
>Yeah? What happened?

JACK:
>Ricky got thrown outta the car. Kinda bad shape.

>*The COP looks at RICKY on the ground.*

COP:
>What's that?

JOHNNY: *dazed*
>She gave him — the scarf —

COP: *turning to him*
>Whudjuh say, son?

>*Silence.*

JACK:
>He's takin' it pretty hard, officer. They're close buddies!

COP:
>Anybody phone the ambulance?

DEBBIE LOU:
>Flora went back to call from the house.

>*JOHNNY kneels to take the scarf from RICKY.*

COP:
>Hey, what do you think *yer* doin'?

JOHNNY:
>Taking this.

COP:
>Don't touch nuthin'. That hanky might be evidence.

>*JOHNNY reacts to this and takes the scarf, putting it inside his shirt and moving away.*

COP:
>You heard — put that back!

JACK:
>It's awright, officer. He should have it — sentimental value. Ricky and him were really tight.

DEBBIE LOU:
> Here's the ambulance!

JACK:
> You guys give the policeman a hand lookin' after
> Ricky. I'm gonna take this boy home — he's really
> shook up. Roy'll give yuh the story. Okay, Roy?

ROY:
> Sure, I'll give yuh all the dope.

> > *ROY and the COP and DEBBIE LOU carry
> > RICKY off. The instrumental music for "The
> > Cheatin' Aria" begins. JACK takes JOHNNY
> > over to the side of the road where they sit.
> > JACK takes out his mickey of whiskey and they
> > drink.*

JOHNNY:
> It's true . . .

JACK:
> Whudjuh say?

JOHNNY:
> You were right.

JACK:
> Right about what, old buddy?

JOHNNY:
> Once they get their hooks into you —

JACK:
> You said it!

JOHNNY:
> They tear you apart!

JACK:
> No listen, John, you got it all wrong!

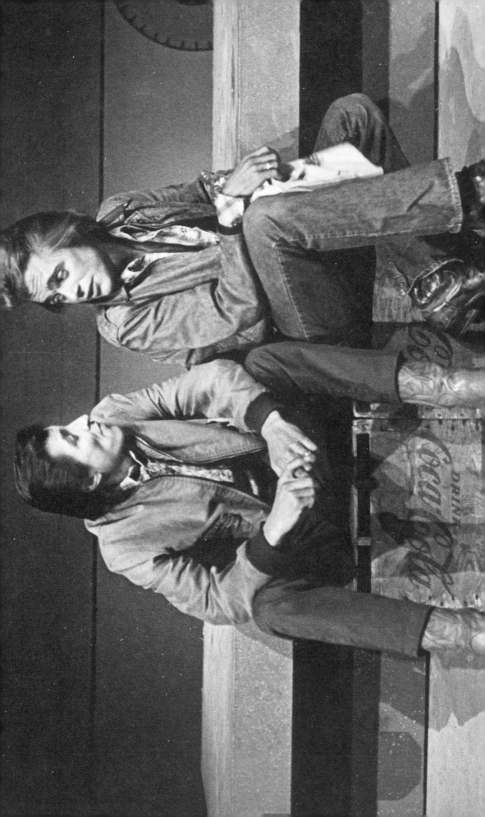

JOHNNY:
>Eh?

JACK:
>You're just dreamin' alla this up.

JOHNNY:
>It's no dream.

JACK:
>Well, I can't believe it! Other women, yeah — they might be rotten to the core — but not *Kathy*. She's too good.

JOHNNY:
>That's what I thought.

JACK:
>Yeah — too good.

JOHNNY: *taking out the scarf*
>Jack — my mother *gave* it to her.

JACK:
>Zatta fact?

JOHNNY:
>And my grandmother gave it to her! It belonged to the women in my family for — generations!

JACK:
>Yeah — the wimmen.

>>*A pause.*

>Always the wimmen.

>>*JACK begins to sing "The Cheatin' Aria."*

JACK:

> *You made your bed, you gotta lie in it.*
> *You got a pillow just to cry in.*
> *You come into this world just to die in it.*
> *Women are the cause of it all.*

> *I seen it happen to all my friends.*
> *One by one they found it out,*
> *That women love to cheat and lie.*
> *It's a cryin' shame without a doubt.*

> *Now Kathy's different, she's good as gold.*
> *It's the other ones you gotta watch.*
> *They'll play around without thinkin' 'bout you*
> *And act like saints when they get caught.*

JOHNNY:

> *I won't let it get me down, Jack.*
> *I figgered out it's all a line.*
> *I know women love to torture us,*
> *Now I know it happens all the time.*

JACK:

> *Yeah Kathy's fine, you're a lucky man.*
> *Don't ever worry about her bein' true.*
> *Oh she may slip up, once or twice,*
> *But she'll come crawling back to you.*

JOHNNY;

> *She wasn't like all them other girls,*
> *Drivin' me crazy with her runnin' around.*
> *Now I see she was laughing at me.*
> *All that time I really was the clown.*

JACK AND JOHNNY:

> *You made your bed, you gotta lie in it.*
> *You got a pillow just to cry in.*
> *You came into this world just to die in.*
> *Women are the cause of it all.*

JACK: *getting up*
Come on, I got another mickey under the seat. One
more for the road — eh?

> *They go out as the lights fade. The lights come
> up on the bedroom. KATHY is in her night-
> gown waiting anxiously for JOHNNY. She
> sings "The Willow Song" à capella.*

KATHY:

*The poor soul sat sighing by a sycamore tree,*
*Sing all a green willow,*
*Her hand on her bosom, her head on her knee,*
*Sing willow, willow, willow.*
*The fresh streams ran by her moans,*
*Sing willow, willow, willow,*
*Her salt tears fell from her and softened the stones,*
*Sing willow, willow, willow.*

*Sing all a green willow must be my garland,*
*Let nobody blame him.  His scorn I approve.*

*I called my false love but what said he then?*
*Sing willow, willow, willow,*
*If I court more women you'll couch with more men,*
*Sing all a green willow.*
*We found our vows drifting like leaves in the wind,*
*Sing willow, willow, willow,*
*And now who is able to gather them in?*
*Sing willow, willow, willow.*

*Sing all a green willow must be our prayer,*
*Restoring the tenderness we once did share.*

*My love turns away when I whisper his name,*
*Sing willow, willow, willow,*
*Now I weep without solace in shadows of pain,*
*Sing all a green willow.*

*Sing all a green willow must be my plea.*
*Such love is not simple.  Please come home to me.*

*She lies down on the bed. JOHNNY enters,
distracted. KATHY descends from the bedroom.
The instrumental music for "The Die Aria"
begins.*

KATHY:
> Johnny?

JOHNNY:
> Yeah.

KATHY:
> Where have you been?

> *A pause.*

> I was so worried!

JOHNNY:
> Were you?

KATHY:
> Of course I was. I've never seen you like that before.

JOHNNY:
> Like what?

KATHY:
> So — violent.

> *Silence.*

> It looked like you were going to *hit* Ricky —

JOHNNY:
> You worried about him?

KATHY:
> Then taking off on that stupid race — both of you
> *drunk*. Leaving me behind in that — madhouse!

JOHNNY:
> Madhouse.

KATHY:
> That wasn't a party — it was a circus!

JOHNNY:
> Yeah.

KATHY: *pausing*
> Sweetheart, has something happened I don't know about?

JOHNNY:
> Yeah, something happened. To Ricky.

KATHY:
> He isn't — hurt, is he?

> *A pause.*

> Johnny?

JOHNNY:
> In the hospital.

KATHY:
> But —?

JOHNNY:
> — *Why?* You wanta know why?

> *A pause.*

KATHY:
> Oh! No!

JOHNNY:
> That's right!

KATHY:
> Johnny — I was *dancing* with Ricky — only dancing!

JOHNNY:
> Dancing with Ricky.

KATHY:
> He's only a — friend!

> *A pause.*

> Don't you realize — there's nothing *wrong* with that?

> *A pause.*

> Johnny, we *agreed* before we got married that we'd never try to possess each other! We have to be *free* — to have our own friends and — interests!

JOHNNY:
> "Interests!"

KATHY:
> *I* wouldn't be jealous if *you* danced with somebody else. It's the only way it'll work. Don't you see?

> *He gestures her toward the bedroom. She sighs.*

> Okay. It's been a long day. We've done too much talking already.

> *She takes his hand. He removes it and pushes her ahead of him toward the bedroom.*

> You know, I'm so scared, when you're not here. I need you — to put me to bed.

JOHNNY:
> I will.

KATHY:
>Promise me you'll always be here to put me to bed, Johnny.

JOHNNY:
>I promise.

>>*They ascend to the bedroom where they sing "The Die Aria." The lighting effects follow the song.*

JOHNNY:
>*Now snuff out the candles*
>*And let the smoke be drawn up*
>*To the heavens waiting patiently above.*
>*My vision is fading,*
>*Darkened by the dying of the light*
>*That once shone in your smile.*

KATHY:
>*Why must we retreat into darkness*
>*To make love as if in shame*
>*When no one can crush this flame?*
>*Look — the light from the stars*
>*Will illuminate two lovers*
>*Seeking out the way.*

>>*JOHNNY closes the curtains.*

JOHNNY:
>*And yet a cloud passing by*
>*Can extinguish that light*
>*Leaving both of us drifting in the dark.*

>>*KATHY removes JOHNNY's jacket.*

KATHY:
>*But you are my world*
>*Revolving in the orbit of these arms*
>*Till we meet the golden dawn.*

JOHNNY:
> *The summer always fades.*
> *The frozen sea of winter*
> *Kills the prairie lily blowing in the sun.*

> *KATHY draws him to the bed.*

KATHY:
> *But life comes full circle*
> *And ice melts into water that*
> *The sleeping lilies drink into life.*

> *Lovers turn to earth*
> *And earth becomes the flowers,*
> *Countless flowers turning to the sun.*

> *You are my sun and earth*
> *And I will journey with you*
> *Through a universe without time or end.*

> *JOHNNY takes out the scarf and strangles*
> *her with it.*

JOHNNY:
> *But if the heavens open*
> *And the planets all collide,*
> *None of us will see the dawn again.*

> *JOHNNY sits up still embracing her as he sings*
> *the last stanza again à capella.*

> *But if the heavens open*
> *And the planets all collide,*
> *None of us will see the dawn again.*

> *There is a knocking at the door. The knocking*
> *is repeated louder. It is FLORA. She enters and*
> *looks around in the semi-darkness.*

FLORA:
Kathy? It's Flora, Kathy!

> *JOHNNY does not hear her. FLORA ascends to the bedroom.*

Kathy?

> *She enters the bedroom.*

Oh uh, 'scuse me. Everythin' okay?

> *A pause.*

Jack just called from the Blacktop. He uh said you were pretty shook up.

> *She looks at KATHY.*

Is she uh sleeping?

> *She sees the scarf.*

How did she —?

> *A pause.*

Kathy?

> *A pause.*

Oh no. Oh — noooooo! *Jack*, what'd you do? Kathy gave the scarf to me!

JOHNNY: *faintly*
Jack?

FLORA: *accusing*
He — killed — her!

A pause.

You *all* killed her!

She backs out in horror and runs off as the
lights fade on the bedroom. The lights come
up downstage as DEBBIE LOU and ROY enter
walking down the street. "The Party Boogie"
begins instrumentally and rises in volume as
they approach the Blacktop Bar.

DEBBIE LOU:
Well, I giss Ricky'll be okay. What are you gonna do
now?

ROY:
I dunno. Wanna stop in to the Blacktop and tell them
about the hospital?

DEBBIE LOU:
The Blacktop? On my night off? You gotta be
*kiddin'*!

ROY:
Alla boys'll be there, Deb.

DEBBIE LOU: *disgusted*
Yeah, all the boys!

ROY: *wistfully*
Might even be some girls.

DEBBIE LOU:
Yeah?

ROY: *realizing this is his last chance*
Maybe I could — escort yuh — to thuh beverage
room?

*DEBBIE LOU looks at him critically.*

DEBBIE LOU:
Oh! Ohhhh — kay, Roy. Then you kin drive me
home — if you're good.

> *ROY gallantly reaches to open the door to the
> Blacktop Bar. "The Party Boogie" instrumental
> opens up to full blast. There is not much action,
> however, as the lights go up on the scene. JACK
> and FILTHY PHIL are getting drunk.*

FILTHY PHIL:
Hey — there's Debbie Lou!

> *He calls to her.*

Over here, Debs! How's Ricky?

> *He grabs JACK.*

Jack — Roy's here!

> *JACK's head goes up, but he is blind drunk.
> He offers only an unintelligible garble. They
> talk and joke as JOHNNY descends into the
> bar.*

Hey — Johnny!

DEBBIE LOU:    *knowing something is wrong*
Johnny?

> *JOHNNY crosses slowly to JACK. JACK sees
> him, grins and rises. The lights begin a slow
> fade.*

JACK:

Johnny, y'ole bo-hunk! Bin waitin' fer yuh. C'mon, say hello to yer good — buddy!

> *JACK crosses to meet JOHNNY and hugs him in an embrace. In slow motion JOHNNY takes out a knife and stabs him in the guts. The others begin to retreat from the bar. The instrumental music for "Lady of the Prairie" begins. JOHNNY drops JACK's body to the floor and returns slowly to Level 1 as the VOCAL CHORUS sings "Lady of the Prairie."*

VOCAL CHORUS:

> *She was a lady of the prairie*
> *And though she thought she'd never marry,*
> *I stole that gal and we left that one horse town.*
> *She said she'd always call me papa*
> *If I would treat her proper*
> *And I swore I'd never let that good gal down.*

> *The lights go up on the VOCAL CHORUS.*

> *My life was a barrel of fun,*
> *My world was in my arms.*
> *She had me up there sittin'*
> *On a cloud that was gold-spun.*

> *JOHNNY sits on the bed and takes KATHY in his arms.*

> *I took her far off to the city*
> *And she was lookin' pretty,*
> *Until I turned one day and saw*
> *That she was gone.*

*Yodelling through one stanza with dobro*
*accompaniment.*

*Well I went downtown to find her,*
*There was another man behind her,*
*And they looked like they was out to have some fun.*

*I said come on home now, sweet momma*
*Back to the arms of your own papa.*
*We'll forget the past and let what's done be done.*

*The lights go out on JOHNNY and KATHY.*
*The light on the VOCAL CHORUS goes to red*
*and fades slowly through the last stanza of the*
*song.*

*Then she melted like a vision,*
*Though I still can taste her kisses.*
*She left me standing in the glaring*
*Evening sun.*

*The stage goes to black. The VOCAL CHORUS*
*yodels the last stanza of the song which fades*
*into the sound of the wind moaning. This sound*
*in turn fades into silence.*

*Cruel Tears* was first published by Pile of Bones Publishing Co., Regina, Saskatchewan.

All lyrics to *Cruel Tears* printed by permission of Shoehorn Music. Music and lyrics are available from Shoehorn Music, P.O. Box 3028, Saskatoon, Saskatchewan.

*Cruel Tears* is also available on record through Sunflower Records, P.O. Box 3028, Saskatoon, Saskatchewan.

(